ORCHIDS ARE EASY
A BEGINNER'S GUIDE TO THEIR CARE AND CULTIVATION

ORCHIDS ARE EASY

A BEGINNER'S GUIDE
TO THEIR CARE AND CULTIVATION

TOM GILLAND

THE GUILD OF MASTER CRAFTSMAN PUBLICATIONS

THIS BOOK IS DEDICATED
TO MY LATE PATERNAL GRANDFATHER,
AS IT WAS HE WHO FIRST INITIATED
MY INTEREST IN GARDENING

First published in 2000 by
Guild of Master Craftsman Publications Ltd,
166 High Street, Lewes, East Sussex, BN7 1XU

© Guild of Master Craftsman Publications Ltd
Text © Tom Gilland 2000

Reprinted 2000, 2001

ISBN 1 86108 145 6

Picture acknowledgements
p44, Geogg Dore/Bruce Coleman Collection; p45 (top left), Kim
Taylor/Bruce Coleman Collection; p45 (bottom right), Alan Stillwell/Bruce
Coleman Collection; p46 (bottom left), Peter A Hinchcliffe/Bruce Coleman
Collection; p46(top right), J S Sira/The Garden Picture Library; p47 (top
left), Hans Reinhard/Bruce Coleman Collection; p47 (top right), Oxford
Scientific Films; p48 (top left), Vaughan Fleming/The Garden Picture
Library; p49, RHS Plant Pathology Department. All other photography
and cover photograph by Tom Gilland.

Designed by Joyce Chester

Cover design by Ian Smith,
Guild of Master Craftsman Publications Ltd Design Studio

Typefaces: Sabon, Frutiger and Lithos
Colour origination by Viscan Graphics (Singapore)
Printed and bound by Kyodo Printing (Singapore) under the supervision of
MRM Graphics, Winslow, Buckinghamshire, UK

CONTENTS

INTRODUCTION

THERE is a common misconception that orchids are temperamental and difficult to grow and it is my aim in this book to demonstrate that, given appropriate growing conditions and maintenance, orchids can be an absolute delight to cultivate. I am the prime example of a plant enthusiast who began with very little knowledge about orchids, yet whose life has been transformed by them! A cursory glance at the facts about orchids will show you how incredible this plant family really is.

With over 25,000 species in existence today and even more hybrid varieties, orchidaceae or, in simpler terms, the orchid family, is one of the largest and most diverse plant species on earth. They are hugely adaptable, thriving in the most extreme conditions and climates and are found on every continent with the exception of Antarctica. They grow along the shoreline at sea level, yet are also found in mountainous regions of over 3,500m (11,480ft) where they are protected by the drier air and rarefied atmosphere. Orchid varieties are equally at home in grasslands as swamplands. Some varieties are even subterranean; their whole life cycle is spent underground, completely oblivious to the interest of the horticulturist.

Given the immense diversity of their habitat, it is unsurprising that there are also great contrasts in their appearance and behaviour. Some varieties grow blooms as little as 1mm in diameter, whereas others grow to two-hundred-and-fifty times that size. It is common for a variety to have only one bloom per plant and another which sways under the weight of a hundred blooms on a single stem. The length of time an orchid is in bloom also varies greatly: some blooms enjoy a brief moment of loveliness, lasting less than a day, while others last many months in perfect condition. The stem of the orchid is just as intriguing: one measures less than 10mm (³/₈in) tall while another reaches to over 2m (6ft) high.

Of the immense variety of orchid species that are known today (and many new ones are discovered every year), there are around fifty native to Great Britain. Many have common names which have developed out of an orchid's particular characteristics or associations: Bee orchid, Monkey orchid and Frog orchid are just a few charming examples. Many have lovely, delicate blooms and, given the right conditions and encouragement, can be successfully grown in a domestic garden. A number of varieties grow in temperate climates, but most originate in tropical regions, for example in Asia and South America. They are selective about their habitat, but are incredibly adaptable. They grow as terrestrials, in the ground; as epiphytes and saprophytes, which are supported by living and fallen trees respectively and lithophytes, which grow on rocks. Some varieties are edible: vanilla essence is extracted from the long, fleshy seed pod of the *Vanilla planifolia*, or more commonly, the Vanilla orchid.

The history of the plant's discovery and its cultivation in Europe is a little over two hundred years old. It has only been in the last fifty or sixty years that they have gained wider interest and accessibility. Until this time, the orchid was the preserve of the wealthy, European plant enthusiast who was able to pay large sums of money to plant hunters for single examples of exotic varieties. In the Victorian period plant hunting was a passion verging on mania.

Although some species are rare because of their extremely localized distribution, it is largely thanks to the activities of ruthless plant hunters that many species are now extinct. In some parts of the world, whole areas of jungle were destroyed following plant foraging expeditions to discourage other plant hunters from collecting the same variety, thereby ensuring the exclusivity of the owner's collection. Tragically, most of the plants never reached Europe. Many collected from high altitudes perished because they were not climatized to the heat levels at low altitudes, while many of those that did survive perished on the long sea journeys.

Those orchids which did successfully reach their destination were cultivated in large orchid houses and maintained by specialist staff. Today, there is little requirement for this level of attention. With increased levels of automation, it is relatively easy to keep an amateur collection. Orchids do not require any more attention than other varieties of greenhouse plants, as long as consideration is given to their growing conditions which should, as far as possible, reflect their natural climate. This means that growers should not attempt to cultivate warm house and cool house orchids together, although it is possible to cultivate a range of intermediate house varieties under the same conditions.

As you will see in the A–Z of Orchid Species section, there is an immense range of orchids to grow to suit all tastes, budgets and growing conditions. I guarantee that once you have familiarized yourself with them, you will soon be seeking out varieties to cultivate in your own greenhouse.

THE ESSENTIALS

IN most parts of the world where orchids are cultivated in a domestic environment, it is necessary to rely upon key pieces of equipment and materials in order to maintain satisfactory growing conditions in as automated a fashion as possible – after all, very few of us can expect to maintain the greenhouse all day, every day of the year. In this chapter, therefore, I advise you on the essentials for orchid growing, whether that be which greenhouse to buy or form of heating to install, while also offering alternatives so that you can adapt what you buy or make to your own constraints. I also address the smaller items that are particularly useful, from netting to pots.

THE GREENHOUSE

Although many people successfully grow orchids indoors as houseplants, it is advisable to buy or construct a greenhouse for your collection so that you can maintain and monitor their growing conditions more accurately. There are any number of greenhouses on the market to choose from

A greenhouse is more cost-effective if properly insulated

and it is important to choose the right one for your needs. When researching the market, keep the following factors in mind to help you decide which is the best one for you.

Budget

Perhaps the most important decision you need to make relates to your budgetary constraints. Aside from the initial outlay for the greenhouse, there are costs you may not have considered, for example the extra cost of electricity to heat your greenhouse and to run automated pumps and watering systems.

Selecting a suitable greenhouse

Additionally, you must consider the amount of time you can spend on maintaining your greenhouse, the space you have in your garden and how many plants you wish to cultivate. These factors will crucially affect the size of greenhouse you buy. It is, for example, very difficult to control the conditions in a greenhouse smaller than 2m x 2.5m (80 x 100in); it can quickly become like an oven when the sun is shining. The larger the greenhouse, the easier it is to control heating, humidity and ventilation.

Contrary to what you might expect, a greenhouse entirely made of glass is not ideal for orchid growing. A lot of heat is lost through the glass which increases your costs and makes your growing conditions less predictable. The most suitable greenhouse is one with some form of cladding around the base on every side, preferably to staging level. The cladding can be constructed from brick, wood or other materials. If you are adept at building work you might like to try constructing this section yourself; alternatively, hire a builder to do it for you or buy your cladding from one of the many greenhouse retailers.

At the same time, consider what kind of frame you require. A wooden frame is preferable to an aluminium one for a number of reasons; it retains heat better than the aluminium variety, it is easier to install insulation and mount shades (aluminium frames are notoriously difficult in this respect) and finally, it is aesthetically more appealing. There are obvious disadvantages, however; it is more expensive to buy and requires fairly regular maintenance.

Choosing the best position in your garden

Once you have selected your greenhouse, the most important decision is where to position it in your garden. If you have a small garden, you may be restricted in your choice of position and will have to make the best of the available conditions. The ideal location is a sheltered, sun-dappled spot, where your plants can enjoy the heat emanating from the sun, away from shade and cool, blustery winds which force up your heating costs. It should also be clear of trees and garden furniture which might cause damage in high winds.

INSULATION

It is well known that to raise the temperature in your greenhouse by just 3°C (5°F), doubles the cost of your heating bills. It is, therefore, highly desirable to install some form of insulation to protect against variance in temperature and unnecessary costs. There are a number of ways to achieve this, depending upon your budget and the solidity of the structure of your greenhouse. Double-glazing, for example, is effective but costly and heavy; few greenhouses are capable of withstanding its additional weight. If you purchase or build a greenhouse with cladding on every side you already provide some form of insulation against the cold without sacrificing the quality of light to your plants. However, there are other forms of insulation which can further improve the conditions in your greenhouse.

Polystyrene

Many orchids do not require high levels of light, therefore insulating panels or sheets of polystyrene are an attractive, lightweight option. The joy of this material is that it keeps the greenhouse warm in winter and cool in summer. If you choose this form of insulation, buy sheets approximately 2.5cm (1in) thick which provides good insulation while also allowing enough light to penetrate. If you have a wooden greenhouse, you can mount the sheets by simply pinning them to the frame. If you have an aluminium greenhouse, cut the sheets slightly larger than the area you wish to insulate and then squeeze the edges of the sheets in place between the struts which will fix them securely. Whichever greenhouse you choose, install the sheets on every side, all the way up to the guttering. If you wish, mount additional sheets above this height on the side facing north and into the prevailing wind.

Polythene

There are two types of polythene available to insulate your greenhouse: the plain sheet variety or bubble polythene. Many growers prefer the former, but I find that just as double-glazing provides an extra layer of insulation to the windows of your home, the trapped air in the bubbles of bubble polythene provides extra insulation to your greenhouse. Additionally, the larger the bubbles, the better the insulation. To fit your polythene to a wooden greenhouse, pin securely to the frame. If you have an aluminium greenhouse, you can buy special clips which fit in the grooves of the aluminium struts. There are a couple of things to note as you fit your polythene. First, ensure that you keep it taut to discourage condensation forming and falling onto your orchids as this can lead to fungal rot. Second, cut away sections of polythene from the air vents so that fresh air can circulate around the greenhouse and excess heat escape. I normally fit polythene over the vents in winter and remove them in summer when extra ventilation is useful. Some growers recommend replacing the polythene every year, but if, in the autumn, you ensure that it is thoroughly cleaned and maintain it properly

These special clips help to secure the polythene to the frame of the greenhouse

throughout the year, it should last several years, although the quality of light will gradually diminish over time.

If you use bubble polythene in conjunction with polystyrene, you will make a substantial saving on your heating costs. It is worth noting that by insulating your greenhouse in this way, it will actually be less expensive to keep an intermediate house than an uninsulated cool house. (I will explain these terms in detail in the following chapter.)

ELECTRICITY

Aside from the greenhouse, probably the most useful item you require is electricity! There are immense advantages for both you and your plants if you can afford to have it professionally installed into your greenhouse. An electricity supply means that heating your greenhouse is clean and easy to manage: you can have lighting, fans for air circulation, pumps for automated watering and humidity systems. There is only one cause for concern you should consider: having a power cut. If you do have a breakdown in power, it takes very little time for your plants to flounder. I would strongly recommend, therefore, that you set up a series of back-up systems for each function in your greenhouse. I would also suggest that you buy a battery-powered temperature alarm which you can install into your bedroom. If the temperature falls below a certain level, the alarm sounds and you can then put your back-up systems into operation as a temporary measure.

If you are concerned about the cost of installation, there are ways of preparing the groundwork to save money without compromising safety. Before you begin any work, consult your electrician and agree on the required course of action. The first thing you will need to do is dig a trench to hold the cable. Once you have agreed an outlet point

for the electricity from the house, dig a trench approximately 50cm (20in) deep where the electrician will lay the cable in a protective covering such as alkathene water pipe, to protect against accidents when you are gardening. You can further help by constructing the panel to hold the sockets, switches and fuse box. Agree on its size and where holes for the cables need to be gouged. Plywood is a good choice of material as it can be screwed easily to greenhouses with wooden frames or attached with special bolts which fit neatly into the grooves of an aluminium frame. When the electrician fits the sockets, remember to keep separate the 13-amp fuse for heating and the 5-amp fuses required for other electrical equipment.

HEATING

The primary means of heating your greenhouse are by electricity, gas, oil and solid fuel. These vary in expense, maintenance requirements and safety levels. Whichever source of heating you choose, it must be capable of maintaining a constant temperature in the greenhouse regardless of the temperature outside. As I have already mentioned, you should always have a back-up heating system to avoid damaging your orchids if you have a power cut. If, for example, your main heating source is electricity, install a bottled gas system as a back-up. You should maintain it as thoroughly as your main heating system to ensure that it performs adequately in the event of a crisis.

Electric heating
Fan heating
Once electricity is installed, there are a number of heating units you might choose. The most common form of electric heating is a fan heater developed specifically for the greenhouse. Its principal benefit is to circulate

SAFETY TIPS

Safety is a key consideration when you use electricity in a wet environment. To maintain a safe greenhouse, consider the following:

1 Install circuit breakers.

2 Provide some form of protection to your electricity panel and other electrical equipment. The best method is to mount a sheet of glass, perspex or, if you have one, an old window frame over or in front of it. Alternatively, though not ideally, you can hang a sheet of polythene over it, being careful to avoid contact with the panel.

3 To protect your heater from moisture, particularly if you use sprinklers, place a wooden board onto the staging and hide the heater beneath.

4 Install lighting! It may sound obvious, but having electric light enables you to see properly as you work and avoid accidents.

5 Whichever lighting you install, for example fluorescent strip-lighting, fix it above your sprinkler system and remember to protect it with a waterproof fitting.

Electricity panel

warm air around the greenhouse, keeping the temperature consistent. If situated at ground level, the warm air is directed along the length of the greenhouse and convection enables it to rise, thereby evenly distributing warm air around the plants.

Tubular heating

An alternative method is tubular heating which requires separate installation. The problem with this method is that the air heated is localized, thereby creating an imbalance in the greenhouse temperature. Additionally, once the warm air rises to the roof of the greenhouse, it is lost through the glass which is a terrible waste of resources. To distribute the air more evenly you will need to purchase a fan.

Thermostat control

If you install an electric heater, you can control its temperature and timing by means of a thermostat. A thermostat is invaluable, but occasionally you will need to check that the coils are functioning properly. To do this, turn it up so that the heater is working at its optimum and check that the heating coils all glow with heat. If one or two are not, they will not radically affect the health of the plants unless the outside temperature plummets to below freezing, but it is advisable to replace them for long-term effectiveness and to keep a spare thermostat and heating coil in case of emergency.

Gas

There are two forms of gas heating: bottled and mains gas. Mains gas is almost as easy to use as electricity, but bottled gas is by far the most common in an amateur greenhouse. If you install a gas heater, place it in an open area, away from any flammable materials, for example polystyrene or polythene insulation. You should avoid positioning it directly underneath your plants as they will suffer from the heat and rising fumes. Gas heaters give off carbon dioxide gases which are beneficial, but they also give off others which are harmful and must be vented. If they are not, the plants will quickly show signs of distress: flower buds drop and the plants begin to turn an ugly yellowish hue. While you should always keep a bottom vent open to ensure an oxygen supply to your gas heater, it is advisable to have an additional ventilator slightly open, even on the coldest nights, to combat these fumes. Gas heaters also produce water vapour, so you will need to keep a close eye on condensation problems.

Like the electric variety, the gas heater can be thermostatically controlled. If using bottled gas, fit two bottles at a time with an automatic switching valve. Once the gas from one bottle is emptied, the valve automatically switches to the other. This is very helpful if the gas happens to empty overnight, but you will, of course, need to replenish the first when necessary so that you do not find yourself without gas altogether. If you choose to use gas as your main source of heating, a paraffin heater provides a suitable back-up system.

Oil

Oil-fired heaters are normally fuelled by paraffin. They often suffer the same disadvantages as gas heaters: fumes, oxygen supply and water vapour. They do not normally have thermostatic controls and are less convenient. Your fuel tank will need to be large enough to be left unattended. In addition, if you do not keep the wick well-trimmed, the flame produces sooty smoke. This heater is not really suitable as your main heat source, but is a good back-up system.

Solid fuel

Many years ago, solid fuel heating was the main source of heating in the greenhouse. A water boiler was housed in the brickwork at the back of the greenhouse and water was fed around the structure through cast-iron pipes which created an evenly heated environment. This system provided a good source of heat and if the pipes were sprayed with water, a good level of humidity, too. However, it was a labour-intensive system: the boiler required stoking with fuel three or four times a day and the ash had to be disposed of elsewhere. Consequently, this system is rarely used today. However, if you happen to have a greenhouse which still has a functioning water boiler and you spend most of your time at home, it is worth maintaining it. I would advise other growers to install another source of heating.

WATERING

Watering orchids is as much a case of watering the air as watering the orchids. It is essential to keep the humidity high in your greenhouse to minimize the transpiration of water from the leaves of the plants, thereby ensuring that water absorbed through the roots is kept at a minimum.

You can use mains water, or preferably, rainwater. If you use mains water, you will have to feed a supply from the mains to the greenhouse and install a storage tank to give the water time to reach the same temperature as the air in the greenhouse. If you use rainwater, you must first collect it in a water butt and then store it. When it rains, the water runs off the roof of your greenhouse and into the water butts. You can then transfer it into another butt or tank inside the greenhouse. Aside from supplying water when you need it, your water butt or tank absorbs heat during the day and releases it at night thereby maintaining a balance in temperature in the greenhouse, in much the same way as a domestic storage heater.

Manual watering

This is the simplest, but most labour-intensive method of watering and entails watering by hand with a watering can or hand sprayer. You will need to water both the compost and wet the floor of the greenhouse to maintain humidity levels.

Automatic watering

There are a number of automatic watering systems you can buy. It is best to avoid the trickle irrigation method because the loose, open nature of many orchid composts means that the water passes through it too quickly to ensure that the roots of the orchids are well-watered.

If you choose to draw on your mains supply, you must install copper piping to ensure that your watering system is able to withstand high pressure. This is an effective method and you can automate it with the addition of a timer or humidistat. With a timer you can predetermine your watering schedule which means that it will water whether the plants require it or not, whereas a humidistat only waters when the humidity level in the greenhouse falls below a set value.

If you choose to water your plants from a rainwater supply, you must install a pump to ensure that there is enough pressure to work the system. You can choose either a submersible pump or one which you place outside the water butt or tank. It works by pumping water from the supply through a pipe with nozzles attached at set intervals along its length from which the water sprays the plants and waters the floor.

You must periodically check the water levels in the container in case it runs out unattended. This is not simply because your plants will suffer; if water levels drop, the pump may

Overhead irrigation

burn out! It is advisable, therefore, that you familiarize yourself with the speed at which the water levels fall so that you can determine how to set the timer's watering schedule to maintain adequate water levels.

AUTOMATIC HUMIDITY SYSTEM

You can maintain humidity either by using the watering systems above or with a separate humidifier.

The humidifier works by sending out a very fine jet of water, rather like steam from a kettle, the difference being that the 'steam' from a humidifier is cool. It can be very helpful: it means that you do not need to manually dampen the floor of the greenhouse every couple of hours, although you are required to top up the water level once a day.

During the summer, it is advisable to couple its work with further dampening to counteract the heat which escapes and humidity which is lessened when the ventilators are open.

STAGING

There are two main types of staging you can buy: those with a solid base and those with a galvanized mesh base.

Solid bench staging

A solid bench can be a satisfactory method of providing staging for your plants, though there are a number of disadvantages. It is a matter of maintaining it properly and being aware of the problems. With a solid bench you can insert capillary matting which will not keep the orchids moist, but will help increase the humidity around the plants. If the bench is stable, you can fill it with gravel and keep it damp to increase humidity levels further. All these materials will need to be cleaned thoroughly at least twice a year to remove fungal spores and pests such as slugs. To avoid clogging the plants with excess water and to encourage drainage, it is helpful to drill holes at short intervals into the solid base. The main disadvantage of solid bench staging is that it reduces the circulation of warm air around the plants as it rises from the heater to the roof. Additionally, it encourages an uneven temperature in the greenhouse which is not a healthy environment for your plants.

Galvanized wire mesh staging

Galvanised wire mesh staging is vastly preferable to solid staging. It allows water filtering through the orchid compost to drip onto the greenhouse floor which, as it evaporates, contributes to humidity levels. Wire mesh staging also allows additional light through to the greenhouse floor enabling you to grow other plants successfully below, for example ferns. It also enables the free flow of air around the plants, an even temperature and prevents the build-up of dead plant material.

VENTILATION

Good ventilation is crucial for a healthy greenhouse. It emulates the environment at the forest canopy where the orchids enjoy constant air movement. Ventilation is, therefore, required to circulate fresh air and thereby counteract the dead air resulting from insulation. Without it, plants have a tendency to retain moisture which can cause fungal problems.

Ventilators

It is advisable to install air vents at the base to draw fresh air in and at the top of the greenhouse to vent stale air out. By way of an example, a 3m x 2.5m (9¾ x 8¼ft) greenhouse should have at least three roof vents and three

Your greenhouse should have at least one roof vent

base vents. Your greenhouse will suffer some heat and humidity loss, but it is a necessary sacrifice to maintain the circulation of fresh air. Fit your ventilators with fine mesh or mosquito netting to discourage pests.

Roof ventilators

Roof ventilators can open and shut manually or automatically. I heartily recommend the latter. Automatic roof ventilators are not powered by electricity, but by means of a hydraulic system. Hydraulic fluid is contained in a cylinder which as it heats up, expands, forcing an arm upward and, as it cools down, contracts, thereby lowering it again. It is not an expensive piece of equipment and it can prevent plants overheating in summer or freezing in winter. You need not fit all roof vents with the automated system, but at least one and preferably two.

Louvre vents

Louvre vents consist of slats of glass which fit together in a hinged unit which you can fit at the base of the greenhouse. As with roof ventilators, the louvre vents operate manually or automatically and follow the same principle. It is advisable to fit at least one.

Louvre vent

Automatic roof vent

Automatic louvre vent

Fans

Orchids like a humid atmosphere, but not a stale one. Many epiphytic orchids grow high in the forest canopy where they enjoy continual air movement and you must replicate this environment in the greenhouse. Fans are, therefore, a great aid. Whether the oscillating or fixed variety, they keep the air circulating over the orchids and the temperature constant, keeping them dry and discouraging the stagnant conditions favoured by fungal diseases. You should install a fan near the roof out of the way of the automatic watering system and at the base of your greenhouse, but if your heat source is an electric fan heater, operate just the one at the top of the greenhouse and, as long as it is run continuously, you may dispense with a second.

Overhead fan

Netting provides an adequate form of shade for your greenhouse

Shades

Shades are required most of the year with the exception of winter. They are required less to reduce light levels than to keep temperatures in the greenhouse within tolerable limits. Without shades, the temperature in the greenhouse can soar above 35°C (95°F). It is best to install shades on the outside of the roof to prevent the heat permeating the glass. If installed inside, the heat is difficult to vent and will affect the temperature.

Blinds

Lath roller blinds provide perhaps the best form of shade, but they are also the most expensive and require a little effort to install. They are normally made from thin strips of wood hinged together and should be mounted to the roof of the greenhouse via a raised rack.

This provides protection to the plants from the sun without risking damage to the glass roof of the greenhouse, a serious consideration in bad weather. Very few amateur greenhouses have automated roof blinds, but if you can afford it, it is worth installing one. The roof blind raises or lowers by means of a pulley system which you connect to an electric motor run by a photoelectric cell. This means that the blinds respond spontaneously to alterations in the weather: when it is sunny, the blinds automatically lower and when overcast, they raise.

Netting

If you cannot afford blinds, plastic netting is a very good alternative medium for providing shade as it allows natural light to filter through the glass, emulating the dappled light of the orchid's natural environment. Cheaper netting only lasts a season or two, whereas more expensive varieties, if properly maintained, last for many years. To fix the netting to a greenhouse with a wooden frame is relatively straightforward; it can be affixed by means of pinning or nailing, but with an aluminium frame you will need to buy an appropriate clipping system or a form of netting which has hooks already fitted. It can be mounted and removed in a matter of minutes and is, therefore, very flexible. They are quite expensive, but are guaranteed to last for at least fifteen years.

Paint

If you are working to a budget, painting your greenhouse in a solution of diluted shading paint is the least expensive form of shading you can obtain. In its favour, it is widely available from garden centres and is easy to apply. The best time to use the paint is in spring when the warm weather arrives and your plants require better protection. Do not be confused by its transparent appearance; as it dries it turns an opaque white which reflects back the heat of the sun, thereby protecting the plants yet ensuring that enough light filters through the glass. Paint is, paradoxically, a drawback during cool weather when every ounce of heat is precious. When you are ready to apply the paint, take care to read the instructions carefully as it requires dilution to the correct consistency. This is very important: if the mix is too thick it is particularly difficult to remove in autumn and if too thin, will wash off with the first rainy spell. To apply, paint it on with an ordinary paintbrush and, in

A selection of containers

Dendrobium kingianum suspended from the roof of the greenhouse

autumn, wipe off with a dry cloth to maximize the light and heat once more. If used properly, this method is an effective method of shading, but I strongly advise against it if you collect rainwater into water butts from your greenhouse roof because you then risk contaminating your water supply.

CONTAINERS

Pots

Orchids can be grown in almost any kind of pot, but with varying degrees of success. The crucial factor in selecting the best pot for your orchid, particularly an epiphytic orchid, is whether it allows enough air to circulate around the roots. Plastic plant pots, for example, discourage air circulation which can cause the compost to decompose and result in root-rot. Clay pots, although heavier and more expensive than plastic pots, are more suitable for orchid growing. The clay allows air to permeate through the compost, thereby encouraging a healthy, dry environment for the roots. The most suitable pots for orchid growing, however, are aquatic baskets or those made of strong, plastic wire, which allow air to circulate freely around the roots. The holes in the plastic also successfully accommodate any aerial roots. If using clay pots or plastic aquatic pots, ensure that your plants receive a regular watering to ensure that the compost does not dry out too thoroughly, thereby starving the plant of moisture.

Wooden baskets

Wooden baskets are ideal containers because they are adaptable to different varieties and growing conditions and, although they are commercially available, can be easily constructed in your own shed! You can either display them on the floor or bench of your greenhouse or, with the addition of some strong wire, suspend them from above,

retaining valuable bench space for other tasks. They are, therefore, particularly useful for unwieldy plants of all kinds, like those with a long rhizome between pseudobulbs, aerial roots or members of the Stanhopea family which produce long, flowering spikes that grow downwards and can become trapped. In addition, any plants which prefer warm, light positions will thrive in these containers.

HOW TO MAKE A WOODEN BASKET

First select your wood for the task. Hard woods last longer than soft, but are more expensive to buy and offer the least environmentally effective option. Any reasonably strong wood can be used, for example cedar, although pine is probably the cheapest, most widely available and environmentally friendly alternative.

1 To make the basket, plan the size and shape required for your plant, allowing plenty of room for the compost and roots. Cut 22 strips of wood approximately 13 x 13mm (½ x ½in) thick and to the required length. Drill a hole approximately 15mm (½in) from each end of each strip of wood to make up the sides of the basket and approximately 6mm (¼in) from each end of each strip of wood to make up the base of the basket.

2 To make up two adjoining sides, take a length of strong, preferably rustproof, wire and thread together eight strips of wood, ensuring that you do not use one of those intended for the base by mistake. Allow enough spare length of wire for hanging the basket. Once you have completed this, extend each strip out, one to the left and another to the right, until you have two sides of alternating strips that form a right-angled corner at one end. Repeat these steps to create the opposite corner of the basket. Now slot the four sides together to form a box shape.

Encyclia pentotis in a home-made wooden basket

3 Turn to the wooden strips to make the base of your basket. Taking the first length of wire you threaded, pass it through the hole at one end of each of the base strips until you have threaded every single one and then take the wire up through the holes of each of the four wooden strips at the other end of this side. Repeat this procedure on the opposite side of the basket. You will now have a completed basket shape. The only remaining task is to ensure the wooden strips on the base are positioned equidistantly apart and then firmly secure them by pinning or nailing them down.

4 To line the basket, use sphagnum moss or plastic meshing. Place the orchid into the basket, allowing enough room for the front of the leading growth so that it will be comfortable for at least two or three years without the need for repotting. Pot up the basket as normal and, if the plant is particularly long and narrow, tie in place to stabilize it.

Tree bark

Epiphytic orchids are displayed to greatest effect on sections of non-resinous tree bark, most commonly, but not exclusively, cork, which serves to emulate the plant's natural environment in the wild. This setting is most suitable for those orchids with thick aerial roots and those, for example *Odontoglossum pardinum* and *Coelogyne elata*, which grow pseudobulbs and have a climbing habit. I often suspend my orchids on their bark mounts from the roof or shelves of my greenhouse which makes a beautiful display and releases bench space for other tasks.

Brassia verrucosa on a bark slab

When mounting your orchid onto the bark section, secure it with plastic-coated, rustproof wire which can be removed once the roots have firmly attached themselves to the bark. In addition, mount a small piece of absorbent, natural material, for example sphagnum moss or tree fern, to the base of the orchid to attract and retain moisture as well as add interest to your display.

COMPOSTS

Prior to 1970, many texts written about cultivating orchids supported a preference for osmunda fibre as the potting medium of choice for orchids. This fibre, developed from the roots of a fern, is now prohibitively expensive and difficult to obtain. It also takes a great deal of experience, time and effort to use properly. With the introduction of cheaper, more accessible materials, osmunda fibre is now rarely used. New potting materials are being developed continuously to meet the demands of growers for materials which are easy to use, with a good mixture of air, moisture and nutrients. Today, pine or fir bark-based composts are the most popular modern composts for growing orchids because, unlike other materials, they actually meet these requirements. The beginner will find it easier to buy ready-made compost from local nurseries and garden centres. Experienced growers, however, will probably prefer to mix their own compost using a tried-and-tested formula.

All composts used for orchid growing are composed largely of different-sized bark chips in combination with other ingredients which will help stop the compost from drying out. For example, a fine compost is composed of bark chips which are approximately 4mm (¼in) in size, a medium compost of bark chips which are 10mm (⅜in) in size and a coarse compost of chips which are up to 15mm (⅗in). Other optional ingredients might include:

- perlag or perlite, a good moisture-retaining medium with a loose texture, made from heat-treated volcanic rock. These materials produce dust and I recommend using a protective face mask when handling it
- charcoal pieces, which help to keep the compost from turning sour
- moss peat, another good moisture-retaining medium, although it has a tendency to wash to the base of your container, making the compost soggy
- Dolomite lime, to reduce the acidity in the compost
- rock wool is effective, although I recommend that you wear protective gloves when handling it to avoid irritation to the skin
- gravel
- Hortag (expanded clay granules)

It is always better to start with a well-known compost and if, at a later date, you wish to experiment, then do so – with care. In my opinion, there are few things as disheartening as watching your precious plants suffer because you have potted them in an incorrectly balanced compost, so experiment only in small batches to test whether your new combinations are suitable for your growing regime. Only when you are completely certain your new combinations are effective should you use a new compost on your entire collection.

COMPOST RECIPE

A good, general compost to suit the majority of orchids can be made following this formula:

- 10 parts of medium grade bark
- 5 parts of fine grade bark
- 3 parts of perlite or perlag
- ½ part of charcoal (up to 10mm (⅓in))

If you require a coarse compost, mix 10 parts of coarse bark into the compost. To make a fine compost suitable for seedlings, reverse the medium and fine grade ratio of bark.

CULTURE

TEMPERATURE is the key factor for successful growth in an orchid's environmental conditions or culture and, needless to say, different orchids fit into different temperature ranges. They are, therefore, classified according to their ideal environment, under three separate 'houses': cool house, intermediate house and warm house. The orchids in the A–Z section at the back of this book are listed according to their best environment to guide you when selecting plants to cultivate.

In fact, although you should ideally grow orchids in the most suitable environment possible, they are amazingly resilient and, to a limited extent, will thrive outside of their recommended temperature range. Orchids respond better to a cooler temperature outside of their range than a warmer one and respond least well to extremes of temperature, high or low. The most common plant failure is attributable to a combination of a very low temperature with high humidity which can give rein to all kinds of fungal infections. In winter, therefore, you must be particularly attentive to temperature levels in the greenhouse.

Many growers like to grow what is termed a 'mixed collection', normally those suited to the lower end of their temperature range which is not only easier to manage but less expensive to heat. If you decide to grow a mixed collection of orchids, you must divide your greenhouse into the three separate houses. If your greenhouse is located on an east–west axis, simply divide the greenhouse lengthways into two sections with the warm house facing south by taking a large piece of polythene sheeting, weighted down at the bottom and attaching it to the roof with clips or pins. If your greenhouse is on a north–south axis, simply divide the greenhouse cross-ways instead. Orchids which favour a cool environment should be located in the section facing north and nearest to the entrance of your greenhouse. Orchids which favour an intermediate environment should be located near the main source of heat in your greenhouse, on staging. Finally, those orchids which favour a warm environment should be located above the source of heat near the roof to catch the rising warm air: the temperature can be 5°C (9°F) higher at roof level than at floor level.

Once you have properly divided your greenhouse into houses, it is worth investing in at least two thermometers, preferably the minimum–maximum variety which, literally, records the minimum and maximum temperatures recorded in a set period of time. Place them in strategic locations in the greenhouse so that you can monitor changes in temperature and ensure that they remain relatively constant. These are widely available from garden centres and supply shops.

The cool house

The cool house is normally maintained at a minimum temperature of 10°C (50°F) at night with at least a 5°C (9°F) rise in temperature during the day. An occasional drop to 7°C (45°F) will not affect your plants as long as the atmosphere is kept sufficiently dry. Many of the orchids grown in the cool house originate in high altitudes and are acclimatized to cool, dry, snow-covered conditions for periods of the year. Indeed, the growth of many cool house orchids slows downs and

Coelogyne Corymbosa, a cool house orchid

occasionally, halts, if the temperature rises above 30°C (86°F). Because of this, pay close attention to the weather, particularly in spring when conditions can warm up quite rapidly, sometimes as much as 10°C (18°F) in minutes.

The intermediate house

The intermediate house is normally maintained at a minimum temperature of 13°C (55°F) at night with at least a 5°C (9°F) rise during the day. This temperature suits many more orchids than the cool house, but is less economical because the heating is kept high and required for longer periods. For this reason it is unusual to dedicate a whole greenhouse to growing orchids suited to an intermediate or warm house.

The warm house

The warm house is normally maintained at a minimum temperature of 16°C (61°F) at night with at least a 5°C (9°F) rise in temperature during the day. If you like orchids which favour a warm house environment and you choose to grow them, you will need to apply far greater vigilance to their care than for the cool and intermediate houses. This is because the artificial heat, which needs to be constant, can dry out the atmosphere making it difficult to maintain the required humidity levels. Additionally, although it is necessary to ventilate your greenhouse properly, an icy blast of air is capable of causing a great deal of harm (and sometimes, destruction) to warm house orchids.

WATERING

Watering orchids is a little different from watering other plants and, in my opinion, is the reason why many growers are under the misapprehension that orchids are difficult to grow. Like other plants, orchids do not like to be over- or under-watered, but the former is worse. Indeed, you should only water the plants when they are quite dry. With experience, it is possible to tell which plants need watering and which dry out more rapidly than others from the weight of the pot when you lift it.

Although you can use tap water to water your orchids, it is preferable to use rainwater; mains water can leave unsightly marks on the leaves, particularly if you live in a hard water area. Either way, your water supply should be stored in a container in the greenhouse before watering so that the temperature warms up to approximately that of the greenhouse and certainly not less than 10°C (18°F) cooler than the foliage of the plants, thereby saving your plants a terrible shock. If you connect your water butts to the downflow pipes from the roof of the greenhouse, you can have a constant supply of water to your greenhouse which is the right temperature and readily available. The water used for spraying should not be more than 10°C (18°F) cooler than the foliage of the plants otherwise the soft tissue of the leaves may become damaged and lead to fungal disease.

Unlike other pot plants, orchids are not normally watered from the base. The composition of the bark-based compost is such that a plant might stand in a saucer of water for days and the top half would still be bone dry. The capillary action in bark composts is simply not strong enough to draw the water through to feed the plant. Orchids are, therefore, generally watered from the top.

When watering, ensure that water does not lodge in new growths or flower buds which prevents the plant from drying out properly. In warmer weather, it is best to use the automatic overhead watering system in the morning only, which gives the plants time to dry out before nightfall when the temperatures cool down.

You can water orchids with either a watering can or water sprayer, but I recommend the latter for efficiency. Using a watering can is quicker, but because the water is not absorbed into the compost very well, there is a tendency to under-water. By using a sprayer, water is distributed more evenly over the compost, absorbed more slowly and gives aerial roots a better supply of moisture. Alternatively, you can water established plants by immersion in a bucket or basin of water for up to thirty minutes which gives them a thorough soaking and means they will not require further watering until much later. Do be careful, though, that you do not over-water.

You can water your plants at any time of day, but I find that watering with a sprayer early in the morning when the sun is not yet high in the sky is the most efficient time. This is not simply a preference; in their natural environment, many epiphytic orchids receive most of the day's moisture from the early morning mists and by midday, will have absorbed it and be thoroughly dry. For the health of your plants, it is preferable to introduce and maintain a relatively strict regime of watering which you can adapt according to the season. While during the winter your plants may only require watering once every two weeks, during the summer you may need to water them every day. The only way to judge how much water your plants need is to check their moisture levels every day until you are confident you completely understand their needs.

HUMIDITY

Like temperature, humidity is another key factor in establishing and maintaining a healthy environment for your orchids. Getting the correct levels of humidity for your plants can be tricky to begin with, but with experience will become much easier.

Orchids prefer a relative humidity of 70–85%, which is considerably higher than that favoured by many other plants. This is because orchids absorb moisture through their roots and, since the roots are usually grown in an open compost, the humidity in the air must be high to compensate. This is not uniform, however. During warm weather, when the plants are growing well, the natural humidity levels can drop by as much as 30% so greenhouse levels should be kept high to compensate, but during cooler, wintry days when plant growth is reduced, they can drop a little lower. Do, however, pay attention to these levels during cool weather: fungal infections thrive in this climate. Humidity does not always simply relate to the season; on very cold winter days, if the air is dry outside and your heating is high and constant, the plants may require an increase in humidity to balance the dry atmosphere.

It is worthwhile investing in two humidity meters to check levels at both bench and roof level as there can be an immense difference between them. Depending on your readings, you may only need to compensate those plants at roof level with a light misting of water. With experience, you will be able to judge when conditions are just right; it may sound strange, but an experienced grower can smell good

Growing ferns in your greenhouse helps maintain humidity levels

Easy orchids like *Epidendrum ibaguense,* can be grown under a layer of damp gravel

growing conditions! In the meantime, simply pay attention to the humidity and temperature gauges and to general changes in the weather and season. If your budget allows, I recommend that you buy an automatic misting system controlled by a humidistat which will automatically adapt to any alteration in humidity levels. If you have an automatic watering system to spray the plants and dampen the floor of the greenhouse, the moisture evaporates and increases the humidity levels, too. The only disadvantage is that on those days which begin with sunny weather but turn to cloud later on, the timer will switch on the automatic watering system even though humidity levels remain high. However, this is comparatively less risky than allowing your levels to drop too low which may dry out your plants.

In addition to watering, you can help maintain humidity levels by other methods, for example growing ferns and other compatible plants underneath your staging and by using gravel on the surface of your soil. Some varieties of orchid are tougher than others and will adapt to alterations in humidity, for example *Epidendrum ibaguense* and *Dendrobium kingianum*, both of which will thrive if grown directly in gravel. If you grow your orchids as house plants, you can create a microclimate by placing the pots in troughs which have been partially filled with expanded clay granules such as Hortag. If the granules are kept consistently damp, they will increase the humidity around the plants and thus compensate for the dry atmosphere generated by central heating.

FEEDING

Epiphytic orchids do not receive an abundance of nutrients in their natural environment; the little they do receive is gained from gases rising from decaying vegetation on the forest floor and bird droppings. In greenhouse conditions, therefore, they require little artificial food in addition to the (rather meagre) nutrients they receive from the compost in their pots. There are circumstances when you should feed them, however. When new growths appear, give

Preparing the feed

Spraying your plants with liquid fertiliser benefits the leaves and roots

them a high nitrogen feed at about half the recommended strength, every two or three watering sessions and later, when flower spikes are due to appear, switch to a fertiliser with a high potash content. During winter, when growth is slow, you need only feed your plants every six watering sessions, possibly less. In-between watering, flush your compost with water to prevent a high concentration of salts from building up which can 'burn' the roots of the plants.

For the best results, alternate feeding the compost with spraying the plant foliage with a liquid fertiliser which will benefit the leaves and aerial roots. By using a spray, you protect against over-feeding and wasting excess fertiliser. As with watering, feed the plant foliage in the morning to give the leaves time to dry off before nightfall.

REPOTTING

Frequency

Although it is difficult to establish precisely how often you should repot orchids, I recommend that you repot seedlings and immature plants every few months and mature orchids every two to three years. If you are in doubt, take a look at your plants to see if they seem to be suffering in their current condition: a plant may have outgrown its current pot; the compost may be in a state of decomposition, particularly if you use plastic pots; the bark in the compost may be of poor quality; the plant may be ill-fed or over-watered.

Without making a note of the frequency at which a plant has been repotted, you can easily lose track of which plant was repotted and when. I therefore find it helpful to keep a note for each plant in a dedicated notebook or by affixing a label to the pot with a note of the last repotting date.

Timing

You can repot your orchids at any time of the year with the exception of winter. If you are repotting an immature plant because it has outgrown its current pot, the best time to do so is when the new growth is 4–5cm (1⅝–2in) high and strong enough to survive the upheaval. Equally, if you wait any longer, you may damage new roots. If the plant is not growing very well or the compost appears to be decomposing, you may have to repot the plant before it reaches this stage in its maturity.

Once repotted, do not feed the plant for about six weeks to avoid 'burning' the roots and allow it to dry out longer than usual to encourage its roots to search for moisture and grow. Give it a light misting with your spray to reduce any effects of dehydration that occur during the repotting and drying-out process.

REST PERIODS

Orchids have pseudobulbs to store water and nutrients to help them overcome adverse conditions. At certain times, they go into a voluntary drought season which enables them to rest for varying lengths of time: some rest for a couple of weeks, others a couple of months and still others appear to have no rest period at all. The rest period normally, although not uniformly, occurs at the end of the plant's flowering period. Some orchids, for example the deciduous orchid, Thunia, begins its period of rest just as its leaves begin to shrivel. Resting is particularly important for plants such as *Coelogyne ochracea*, which often produces the most beautiful spiky flowers during this period of its cycle.

The plant's rest period can be a confusing time for the grower, particularly the beginner. The only way to track a plant's rest period is to note when it appears to occur and for how long, by keeping a plant diary or labelling each individual plant with its history. It is also helpful to research this information from literature on the subject in your local library or consult a local orchid growers' society. Once you have established a plant's cycle, you can group it with other plants whose rest periods concur, making it far easier for you to recognize which plants do not require continued watering.

HOW TO REPOT PLANTS

To repot, remove the plant from its current container, gently teasing away the old compost from the roots. If there are any dead leaves, pseudobulbs and roots to remove, do so with a sterilized instrument. In some cases, you may need to destroy the old container to remove a plant. Do not be tempted to salvage the pot if it means risking damage to the roots of the plant – there is always another pot but not necessarily another plant!

Find a clean pot that is large enough to allow another two years' growth. If you are using a plastic or clay pot, place a few pieces of polystyrene, expanded clay granules or gravel into the base; for aquatic pots or wooden baskets you will not require any material for drainage. Fill in with compost, carefully pot the orchid, top up with compost and press firmly into place. If you are using a wooden basket, first line with sphagnum moss or other permeable liner then pot as above. You may need to tie the plant in place to keep it upright. If mounting onto bark, insert a pad of sphagnum moss or osmunda fibre between the bark and the orchid to help retain moisture then tie into place with rustproof wire which can be removed later.

Containers with mixed planting

COMPANION PLANTS

In the early stages of cultivating an orchid collection it is worth considering whether you would like to grow other, compatible plants in the greenhouse. I have already mentioned the beneficial aspects of doing this: other plants can provide shade and increase humidity. Of course, you may simply wish to extend the variety of your display!

The most important factor to consider when selecting compatible plants is that orchids like high humidity, so plants which like a dry environment, for example cacti, will simply not be suitable. Similarly, many orchids also like shade, so those plants which require a lot of light, for example carnations, are unlikely to do well. You can always indulge your other plant passions elsewhere in the home or garden! However, if you are particularly fond of a plant species and its requirements do not clash too much with those of your orchids, there is no reason why the two cannot be cultivated together. If you find the combination is not working, you can either try to adapt the growing conditions slightly to accommodate both species of plant, or transfer the combination plant to a more suitable environment.

Plants which can successfully be grown alongside cool and intermediate house orchids include the following:

- Bananas
- Air plants
- Carnivorous plants
- Dwarf peaches
- Dwarf pears
- Vegetable and bedding plant seedlings
- Fibrous-rooted begonias
- Ferns
- Passion flowers
- Tomatoes
- Pelargoniums

The tomatoes and pelargoniums really represent the limit of what can be grown alongside orchids, but I have in the past produced healthy crops of both, so it is worth an attempt. If you choose to do so, pay attention to the appearance of the fungi *botrytis* and any other problems which occur so that you can resolve them before they escalate. Of the remaining plants in the list, fibrous-rooted begonias and ferns thrive particularly well and will often produce seedlings for you to transplant. While I hope this list is suggestive, it is not exhaustive, so do not be afraid to experiment with other plants which you think might thrive in your greenhouse – simply be ready for the possibility of failure.

PROPAGATION

IT is always a good idea to propagate new plants from your existing collection. Propagation safeguards against the potential loss of a plant from disease or adverse conditions and means that you can afford to exchange plants with other growers to vary your collection. Of course, you might simply wish to extend your collection of a favourite variety too. If you choose to propagate your plants it is reasonable to assume that, whether you propagate directly from the plant itself by division or from seed, you will require a great deal of patience. Many new plants take a long time to grow and even longer to flower.

Vanda cristata, a monopodium

PLANT PROPAGATION

Monopodia

A monopodium is the main axis of growth or stem on a plant, which elongates from the tip and gives rise to lateral branches. Some species, vandas for example, produce small shoots from the base of the mother plant, but this is rare for monopodia.

HOW TO PROPAGATE MONOPODIA

Propagation is relatively easy, but requires great care. Taking a sharp knife, sever the stem of the plant cleanly below the aerial roots then remove the top part of the plant, complete with its own root system, and pot it up in compost.

After a few weeks, you will see the previously dormant buds in the axils of the leaves at the bottom of the original plant begin to appear. After a couple of months these new shoots will develop their own root systems which you can then remove and pot up in compost in the same way as before.

Sympodia

The sympodia form the lateral shoots or branches that emerge from just behind the apex of the main plant, rhizome or rootstock of the old growth, which ceases to grow and dies away. Once established, they form complete plants in their own right. Orchids which have pseudobulbs are an example of sympodia.

There are at least three methods for the propagation of sympodia.

HOW TO REMOVE BACK BULBS

1 First remove one of the old back bulbs, which should be green and healthy in appearance, and dust the severed areas of the bulb and mother plant with sulphur or fungicide to discourage fungal infection. You can buy these from most garden centres.

2 You have two alternatives at this point: you can either pot up the plant or place it carefully in a clear plastic bag with a small piece of moss. To pot up the bulb, take a clean pot containing broken pieces of crockery or terracotta and fill in with compost. Insert the bulb and fill in around the edges with further compost and press gently, but firmly, into place. Alternatively, loosely wrap the bulb in enough moss to ensure that it is covered and place both carefully in a clear plastic bag. The moss provides moisture to the bulb, thereby promoting root growth.

New growth appears from the bulb after a period of about eight weeks, but can take as long as a year. An individual plant normally produces several pseudobulbs before flowering, so new plants obtained by this method will probably take several years to flower. Some genuses, for example Odontoglossum, respond with some reluctance to propagation by this method, whereas Coelogynes and Encyclias grow particularly well. You may well wish to keep this in mind when cultivating orchids.

Encyclia pentotis, an orchid which grows particularly well if propagated from back bulbs

PLANT DIVISION

A successful alternative to propagating from bulbs is to divide large plants into smaller, new plants. The most suitable plants for division are those which may have developed dead centres.

Dead centres occur as the plant grows outwards, leaving the older, inner part of the plant to die. This makes the plant unsightly and therefore suitable for propagation.

1 Remove the plant from its container and gently remove all of the excess compost from around its roots. This means the roots remain unclogged, ready for repotting.

2 Carefully divide the plant into sections, each including at least four healthy pseudobulbs if possible. If it has shrivelled pseudobulbs, dead roots or leaf bracts, remove them.

3 To pot up, follow the procedure above. You can pot up the plants in separate pots or, if small enough, into a single, large pot. Once the new plants are pressed firmly into place, tap the pot on the bench to ensure that there is good contact between the roots and the compost. Roots should not be left suspended in the air.

Although this method is often a successful one, it is not advisable to propagate too frequently from the same specimen plants; they give a far better display of flowers and offer greater resistance to disease and fluctuations in growing conditions if they are given plenty of time during which to establish themselves properly.

HOW TO PROPAGATE FROM DENDROBIUMS

If you wish to propagate from dendrobiums, I find the following method works very well. Dendrobiums produce flowers from nodes which run along the whole length of its cane. If you have a plant which does not, you have a fine opportunity to propagate a new plant.

1 Take a sharp, clean knife and sever the old, leafless cane from the mother plant. Cut it into short lengths, between the nodes, and dust the severed areas with sulphur or fungicide as before.

2 Position the severed cane lengths in a seed tray with the tops facing upwards and fill in with a fine grade of compost. Cover the tray with a piece of glass or clear plastic and place in a warm, light position. Inspect the cane lengths regularly for signs of pests or rot.

3 When the new shoots appear from the nodes on the old canes and begin to tap at the glass or plastic cover, remove it. After about a year, the new plants can be removed from the seed tray and individually potted up. They will take probably three to four years to flower.

Dendrobium infundibulum

HOW TO PROPAGATE FROM ODONTOGLOSSUMS

1 If you are planning to propagate from odontoglossums, wait until spring when new growths appear. Take a knife and cut through the rhizome behind the leading pseudobulb. Do not disturb the plant until new growth appears on the pseudobulb behind the cut area.

2 When new growth occurs, divide the growth and plant into two and repot each individually, following the instructions given above.

Keikis

Some orchid varieties, *Thunia Marshalliana*, for example, propagate by themselves, producing small plants sometimes known as 'keikis'. Once the keikis have established a sufficient root system, they can be cut from the mother plant and potted up separately.

Offset from a *Thunia Marshalliana* specimen

PROPAGATION BY SEED

In a laboratory environment, orchids are raised from seed in a flask using a special culture and cultivated under sterile conditions which offers the plants the best chance of survival. Of course, for many growers, orchids grown from seed are propagated in the greenhouse and, although conditions are not as reliable, they are often successful.

It is a stunning fact that a single orchid seed pod can contain several hundred thousand seeds. This ensures that one of them makes contact with the fungus uniquely suited to that variety of orchid and germinates. Once the seed germinates, the fungus grows in symbiosis with the orchid, providing the necessary nutrients for its continued growth.

HOW TO PROPAGATE FROM SEED

1 To grow orchids from seed already harvested, take a potted plant of the same variety and top up with fine-grade compost. Level the compost so that the seed does not wash away when watered. Sprinkle the fresh seed around the base of the plant. Water the seeds by immersing the container into water, allowing the plant to soak the water up from the base. It can take months before new growth appears.

2 When the seedlings reach 2.5cm (1in) tall, repot them into individual pots – and wait. It can take 5 years for the seedlings to flower.

WATERING NEW PLANTS

Whether you propagate by division or by seed, new plants, like all plants, need regular watering and care. Check new plants and if they seem dry, water them.

PESTS AND
DISEASES

PESTS

Orchids are not as prone to attack from pests as many other plants can be, but they are by no means immune and it is advisable to deal with them before they multiply to save damage to precious plants and reduce the need for poisonous chemicals. I have outlined below the main pests suffered by orchids, against which you should be vigilant.

Slugs and snails

Slugs and snails are the bane of the orchid grower's life. They thrive in warm, humid conditions, just as orchids do, which makes the greenhouse environment very attractive. If you do not keep a close eye on these pests,

Garden snail

they can quickly do a lot of damage to your plants by eating roots, leaves, flowers and new growth. If the latter occurs, a whole year's work, possibly two, may be lost because orchids do not necessarily produce new growth every year. Watch out particularly for 'garlic' snails which are much smaller than other snails and slugs and are, therefore, more difficult to spot.

To control slugs and snails, you can try the following methods, perhaps in combination, to see which you find most effective. If you are not averse to chemical methods, then sprinkling slug pellets in amongst your plants is effective, or alternatively and perhaps less cruelly, use home-made traps, for example what is known as a 'slug pub': a cut-off soft drink bottle buried in the soil up to the rim and filled with beer, into which the slugs fall and drown. It may sound strange, but you can also try to persuade a frog or toad to make its home in your greenhouse; they are extremely effective in reducing a snail or slug population. Finally, I find that the most effective method is simply to inspect your plants late at night when slugs and snails tend to feed. If you wish to let them live – dispose of them, preferably outside of the garden!

Red spider

Although not as persistent as slugs and snails, red spiders can be equally devastating; they quickly swell in numbers and can do quite a bit of damage before you notice you have a problem. If you are in doubt, check the underside of leaves for a layering of silver; if the attack is severe, you will also find a fine, webbing pattern. If left untreated, the plant will certainly suffer and can die.

Aphids

Although aphids are not as common a problem for orchids as they are for many other plants, they can be a nuisance. They tend to attack the flower buds, spikes and very new growth. To counteract the problem, it is normally sufficient to wipe the aphids off by hand regularly, but if you find that they have created more widespread damage, leaving sticky and sooty residue on the plants, then wash off immediately with water. It is not advisable to use insecticides on soft growths or flower buds as they have a tendency to burn the soft plant tissue, damaging it permanently. If the flower buds become badly infested, it is preferable simply to cut off the flower spike rather than allow it to flower because once open, the buds are likely to be distorted.

Red spider mites

To discourage red spider mites, regularly wipe the leaves of your plants with a damp cloth or cotton wool. If you find evidence of the red spider, spray once a week with an insecticide or malathion. If you prefer to use non-chemical methods of control, introduce small, predatory mites into the greenhouse which are harmless to plants but effective in eliminating red spider mites.

These pests generally favour warm, dry conditions although some strains survive marginally damp conditions. To prevent or counteract this problem, keep your greenhouse damp and do not allow it to dry out. During the summer, or in winter when the heating is on, and the plants are in danger of drying out, be particularly vigilant about watering. If possible, install automatic watering or misting systems as discussed. Additionally, plant ferns to help maintain a moist atmosphere.

Black bean aphids

Scale

Scale are not a common problem for orchids, but once they have taken hold on a plant, they can be very difficult to eradicate. Scale are sap-sucking insects with a tough, protective outer coating which makes them very difficult to control with insecticides, although, unfortunately, there is little alternative. If the problem is contained, simply paint the infected areas with methylated spirits then separate these plants from your healthy ones and remove them to another part of your greenhouse. Keep a close watch on the problem in case there are any signs of re-infestation. If, however, you experience a severe attack on your plants, spray them with insecticide at bi-weekly intervals for several months. This should help to alleviate the problem of scale.

Mealy bug

In appearance and ferocity, mealy bugs are very similar to scale. They too are sap-sucking insects which coat themselves with a white, waxy protective film that has a woolly appearance. They normally secrete themselves in the axils or sheaths of leaves. If you experience an attack, try the same methods of eradication as for scale.

Mealy bugs

Woodlice

As any gardener will tell you, woodlice are among the most pullulating of garden pests and are therefore a common problem in the greenhouse. These creatures tend to thrive on decomposing material but will attack plant roots and quicken the decomposition of bark compost. You will notice them at night, particularly if you perform slug and snail

Scale insect in advanced state of fluffyness

Woodlouse

Millipede

control, in which case they can be dealt with by hand. Alternatively, if they become a nuisance, spray them with insecticide or sprinkle slug pellets.

Millipedes

Millipedes are long, thin insects divided into segments, with two pairs of legs per segment. They are differentiated from centipedes which

Vine weevil damage

have one pair per segment. This is an important identification point since centipedes are welcome visitors to the greenhouse because they eat pests whereas millipedes eat only plant tissue. They attack plant roots, causing irreparable damage.

Thankfully, they are easily trapped. To make your own trap, take a large potato, cut it in half and scoop out some of the flesh. Positioned strategically around the greenhouse, these effectively secure the millipedes who simply cannot climb out.

Vine weevil

Vine weevils are small creatures, somewhat beetle-like in appearance, with large antennae. They tend to attack at night, feeding on the leaves and flowers of the orchid and leaving unattractive, jagged patterns in their wake. It is sometimes difficult to distinguish between damage caused by vine weevils and slugs or snails. If you do not see traces of the slime trail left by the latter, you can assume that the vine weevil is responsible. Unfortunately, they are impervious to insecticides, which means that the only certain method of control is to track them down at night and dispose by hand. The single disadvantage of this method is that when the pests are exposed to light in

Vine weevil larvae

the greenhouse (overhead or from a torch), they head for the dark, normally dropping to the floor to hide, so it is advisable to use as little light as you can and to be quick and methodical.

In addition to the adult, the vine weevil larvae are also pernicious. They do a great deal of damage by eating the roots of the plants. They have the appearance of small, white grubs and hide in the compost of the plant's container. If you suspect that your plant has an infestation, remove it from its pot and check the compost.

DISEASES

Orchids, like other plants, do occasionally suffer from diseases of various kinds. To prevent the onslaught of ill-health in your plants, you can help by keeping an hygienic

Keep your plants healthy and vital by maintaining them properly

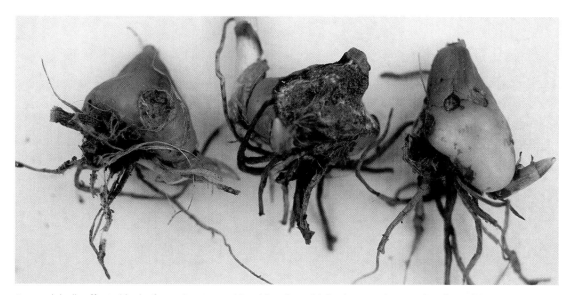

A pseudobulb affected by leaf spotting, caused by either fungal infection or adverse cultural conditions

greenhouse. This means cleaning up leaves, other dead material and decomposed compost regularly and removing pests when they occur. You should also maintain your plants properly so that they remain vital and healthy. Sometimes, however, orchids may appear to have a disease by showing signs of marking or spotting. These are usually attributable to age, particularly on those plants which retain their leaves for several years. Do be judicious when inspecting your plants for signs of ill-health: check any reference material you have before throwing out a plant in case it is perfectly healthy.

Viruses

It is sometimes difficult to establish whether a plant has a virus or not. If a plant shows signs of being unwell, it might be attributable to other factors than its having a virus. However, a definite symptom of a virus is an angular-shaped mottling pattern on a plant's leaves. The only certain way to establish a virus, however, is to send the affected leaves to a professional laboratory for analysis. Unfortunately, this can be costly. If the plant is infected with a virus, it should be destroyed to stop it transmitting to other plants via sap-sucking insects or pruning tools. To reduce the possibility of the latter, ensure that you sterilize your tools between plants. To do this, dip your tool in methylated spirit or pass through a flame. Any flame will do, but a cigarette lighter is possibly the most mobile.

Black or brown spot

This disease is caused by either fungal infection or adverse cultural conditions. It plagues the pseudobulbs or fleshy leaves of the plant, whereby the affected areas turn soft and watery and produce spotting. If you catch the disease early, the affected area can be cut out with a clean knife and the remaining area dusted with sulphur or a fungicide. If the disease is extensive, you should dispose of it to avoid transmitting it to other healthy plants.

QUESTIONS AND ANSWERS

MANY growers, particularly beginners, often find that they have a lot of questions about their collection and about orchid growing in general. In this section I address a few of the most common questions asked and offer, I hope, comprehensive answers. It is obviously not possible to cover everything you may wish to know here, but if you require further information about a problem or have any further questions, consult your stockist or members of your local orchid growers' society.

Odontoglossum Reichenheimii

In what parts of the world do orchids grow?

Orchids are, perhaps surprisingly, adaptable to different climates and thrive on every continent except Antarctica.

How long do orchids live?

Most orchids live for a great many years and, if properly maintained, outlive their owners.

Are orchids parasites?

No, they are not. Some orchid varieties live on trees, but do not live from them. The plant uses the tree as a support but does not extract nutrition from it.

Are orchids difficult to grow?

No. Orchids are just as easy to cultivate as other plants. Most plants, whether houseplants or plants grown in the greenhouse, require care and consideration to survive, so orchids are really no different at all. If you are in any doubt about what kind of care is required, contact your local orchid growers' society and read as much information as possible.

Can I grow orchids from seed?

Yes you can, but if you attempt to do so in a domestic greenhouse environment, it requires a lot of patience; plants can take as long as 5 years to flower. However, orchids grown from seed are normally grown in agar jelly in sterilized jars under laboratory conditions.

Are orchids expensive?

When orchids first became desirable in the Victorian period, they were almost priceless. Today, orchids are accessible to everyone, costing much the same as houseplants.

Masdevallia granulosa has a distinctive chocolate fragrance

Do I need a greenhouse to grow orchids?

No, there are many orchid varieties which can be successfully grown as houseplants. Always read the label or ask advice when buying an orchid to check that it is suitable for growing indoors. Those orchids with many aerial roots are generally unsuitable.

Where can I buy orchids and orchid supplies?

Contact your local orchid society for information.

Are orchids fragrant?

Many, but not all, orchids have a fragrance and these will vary from light, citrus scents to powerful, musky ones. *Masdevallia granulosa* has a distinctive chocolate fragrance.

When do orchids flower?

They can flower at any time of year, but most commonly in late winter and spring.

How frequently do orchids flower?

The frequency of flowering depends on the specific orchid variety. Some flower once a year, others more than once and some flower all year round. Again, consult your literature or orchid society to check which ones flower frequently and which do not.

How long do orchid flowers last?

To a great extent this depends on the orchid variety. Some only last for one or two days whereas Odontoglossum orchids, for example, last for two to four weeks. Paphiopedilums can last for as long as 3 or 4 months.

Odontoglossum Rossii. Odontoglossums favour dappled shade

How often should I water my orchids?

Orchids with pseudobulbs require less frequent watering than those without, because the pseudobulbs act as water reserves which enable them to survive periods of drought. The best way to judge if a plant requires watering is to feel the weight of the pot. To get a feel for the difference between the plant's weight when dry and when wet, test the weight when you water and when it is dry. It is worth noting that more orchids fail due to over-watering than under-watering, so water your plants thoroughly, but not over frequently.

How often should I feed my plants?

Orchids do not usually require much feeding. I recommend you mix a half-strength fertilizer with water once every two to three weeks during the growing season, reducing this to once every two months during winter.

How much light do orchids need?

How much light an orchid requires depends, once again, on the variety. Dendrobiums, oncidiums and cattleyas like lots of bright light, whereas odontoglossums prefer dappled shade and paphiopedilums medium to heavy shade.

How much humidity in the air do orchids need?

Most orchids prefer a humidity range of 70–85%, although they will survive a drop in humidity to 50%.

When is the best time to mist orchids?

Misting your orchids is a good way to keep them hydrated and healthy. When misting, spray on a warm day before early afternoon to give the plants time to dry out before nightfall. If you leave it much later, the damp and low temperatures encourage fungal problems.

Is it a good idea to fan air onto orchids?

It is essential to have a fan in the greenhouse to help maintain a healthy atmosphere. As long as the air is not cold, a gentle breeze is beneficial, particularly for epiphytic orchids which, in their natural environment, grow high up in the forest canopy.

Can I use pesticides on orchids?

You should rarely need to use pesticides on your orchids, and in some cases they can do more damage than good to a plant. If you have problems with aphids and other sap-sucking pests, wash them off with a spray of water. Only in very persistent cases should you use pesticides and, if you do, read the manufacturer's instructions carefully.

Why won't my orchids flower?

If your orchids do not flower, there are a couple of reasons why this might be so. First,

Oncidium Gardneri

it may be due to a lack of light. Plants require light to convert nutrients into energy (photosynthesis) and need a lot of energy to flower. Alternatively, it may be due to temperature. Many orchids require at least a 5°C (9°F) temperature drop at night to initiate flowering. If you have an orchid which normally flowers but has not done so this year, it may be due to abnormal climatic conditions, transplantation, or require repotting.

Why are the flower buds on my orchids turning yellow and dropping off?
The problem of dropping flower buds can be attributed to a number of things. It may be caused by fumes from gas and oil heaters, variations in temperature due to draughts or because the plant has dried out too much between watering sessions.

GLOSSARY
OF TERMS

Adventitious A part of a plant which develops in an abnormal position, for example a root from a node on the stem.

Aerial root A root that has no contact with the growing medium and grows in the air.

Anther The upper part of the stamen in a flower which contains the pollen.

Axil The angle between the upper part of a branch or leafstalk and the stem.

Back bulb An old, leafless pseudobulb.

Bract A leaf-like structure which often grows in the upper angle between a leaf and stem.

Chlorophyll The green pigment in plants that traps the energy from sunlight for photosynthesis.

Column The central structure of the orchid containing the stamens and pistils.

Damping off Any number of fungal diseases arising out of excessively moist conditions which attack seedlings and cuttings, and cause the base of the stem to rot.

Deciduous A plant that sheds its leaves every year at the end of its growing season.

Epiphyte A plant that grows on another plant, but is not parasitic.

Foliar feeding Spraying a plant with a nutrient solution which it absorbs through its leaves.

Fungicide An agent that prevents or destroys fungal disease.

Genus A family of plant species that share similar characteristics.

Hybrid A plant which is the result of cross-breeding at least two different varieties of plant. The hybrid normally combines the best qualities from each parent plant.

Inflorescence 1) The stem of a plant that produces the flower-bearing stalks, 2) the arrangement of flowers on the stalks, and 3) blossoming.

Intergeneric The mobility between two or more genera.

Internode The section of a stem between two separate nodes.

Keiki A Hawaiian term used to describe a plant propagated from an offshoot of another plant.

Labellum The part of the corolla (mass of flower petals) that forms an often lobed lip.

Lead A new growth on a plant.

Lip The non-technical term for the labellum.

Lithophyte A plant that grows on rocks.

Mericlone A plant developed as a result of meristem culture.

Meristem A plant tissue responsible for growth.

Monopodium The stem or main axis of growth from the terminal bud.

Mycorrhiza The symbiotic or parasitic association of a fungus and a plant's roots.

Node A joint on the stem of a plant from which leaves or stalks grow.

Ovary The female part of a flower that develops into a seed pod when fertilized.

Parasitic plant A plant that lives on and gains nourishment from a host plant.

Perlite Heat-treated volcanic rock granules that absorb water and nutrients and can be added to soil and compost as a conditioner. They are sometimes used as an aggregate in hydroponic systems.

Petal Any of the separate parts of the corolla of a flower.

Photosynthesis The production of food by plants using energy from sunlight, carbon dioxide, water and nutrients.

Pistil The female reproductive organ, consisting of the ovary, style and stigma.

Pollen The grains containing the male gametes

borne by the anther for the purpose of fertilization.

Pollination The transfer of pollen from the anthers to the stigma in a flower. There are essentially two mechanisms for pollination, by wind and by insects.

Propagation A means of producing a new plant. This can either be sexual, by seed, or asexual, by taking plant cuttings.

Pseudobulb The bulb-like stems of some orchid varieties.

Rhizome A root-bearing horizontal stem connecting pseudobulbs or upright stems.

Rock wool Also known as mineral wool. A fibrous, soiless growing medium produced by blowing steam or air through molten rock, in much the same way as candyfloss.

Species A group of plants that have one or more common characteristics that differentiate them from another group.

Spike The inflorescence or flowering stem of a plant.

Stamen The male reproductive organ in a flowering plant.

Stigma The tubular part of the ovary which deposits the pollen into the gynoecium.

Stomata Pores in the leaves and stems of plants through which gases and water pass.

Sympodium An offshoot of the main plant which develops from the rhizome of the previous season's growth to become a complete plant in its own right.

Systemic Often used in reference to insecticides. A systemic insecticide is one

Vanda Rothschildiana

which is absorbed into the tissue of the plant, making it toxic to insects and parasites without destroying the plant itself.

Terrestrial A plant which grows in the ground.

Throat In orchids with a tubular lip this is the name commonly given to the gaping lower part of the tube.

Transpiration The evaporation of water from the leaves and stems of a plant.

Velamen The sheath of protective cells around the roots of some orchids.

Virus A submicroscopic infectious organism which increases in the cells of the host causing disease.

A-Z OF
ORCHID SPECIES

IF you plan to start your own orchid collection, or need to know a little bit more about a particular variety, I hope this directory of orchid species will be helpful. It is, necessarily, a selective list of plants not simply because there is a vast range to choose from, but because as a beginner to orchid growing, it is very important to see the successful results of your labour early on; the varieties listed here are chosen for their popularity and ease of maintenance.

Many books on orchids specialize in hybrid varieties because plant breeders tend to prefer the larger, more flamboyant flowers, often at the expense of scent, but I favour the more subtle, delicate varieties with a more powerful fragrance. I make no apologies for the bias towards these latter varieties in the following

section: like all growers, I just love them.

On a technical note, there has been a lot of confusion over the names of orchid genera in the last few years. The Odontoglossum family, for example, has now been divided into three genera: Rossioglossum, Lemboglossum and Osmoglossum. Also a number of varieties originally belonging to the Oncidium family have been temporarily members of the Odontoglossum family only to become Oncidiums again. It is virtually impossible, therefore, to identify accurately which variety belongs to which genera in every single instance, so I have attributed to each the appellation in most common usage. Inevitably, there may be some disagreement about this, but this is welcome: it is all part of the ongoing debate surrounding orchids.

Oncidium papilio ▶

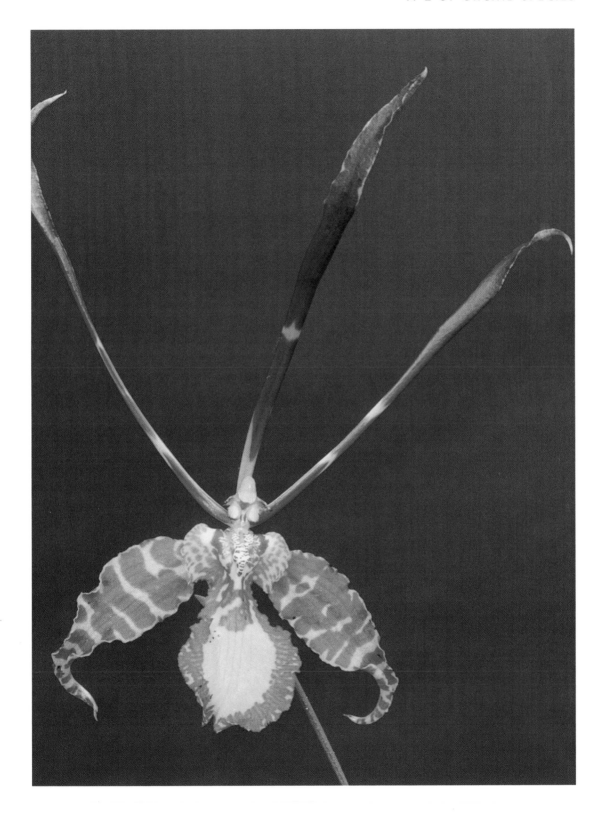

COCHLIODA NOETZLIANA

Native habitat: This orchid is a native of Peru.

Description: The inflorescence has an arching habit, grows up to 45cm (18in) long and flowers in abundance. The blooms can be up to 5cm (2in) in diameter and are a bright brick red, as are the sepals and lip. The pseudobulbs are up to 7.5 cm (3in) high and, with age, tend to form surface indentations. At the top of the bulb a single leaf is produced, up to 25cm (10in) in length.

Flowering season: Summer and autumn.

Cultivation: A medium-grade compost, dappled shade and cultivation in a cool house environment are required.

Propagation: Due to its striking colour, this orchid is a favourite of breeders who use it to produce Odontoglossum, Oncidium and Miltonia hybrids. It makes a good specimen plant and, when in flower, gives a superb show.

Synonym: *Odontoglossum Noezlianum.*

COELOGYNE CORYMBOSA

Native habitat: This orchid originates from the Himalayas where it grows at altitudes of 1,500 to 2,500m (5,000 to 8,250ft).

History: It was discovered by Joseph Hooker in Sikkim in 1849.

Description: The flowers have an arching habit and grow to a height of 15cm (6in), each producing two to four flowers. The fragrant flowers can be up to 5cm (2in) in diameter and are white with yellow markings and an orange centre. The pseudobulbs are up to 5cm (2in) high with two rather tough leaves at the top which grow to 12.5cm (5in) long.

Flowering season: The flowering season is spring when the flower spikes appear from the centre of new growth.

Cultivation: A medium-grade compost, light shade and cultivation in the cool house are required.

Propagation: This plant bulks up quickly and makes a good a specimen plant.

Synonyms: It has no synonym, but is often confused with *Coelogyne ocellata*, which has smaller flowers and a wider lip.

COELOGYNE CRISTATA

Native habitat: This orchid is a native of the Himalayas where it grows at altitudes of 1,500 to 2,000m (5,000 to 6,600ft).

History: It was first formally mentioned in *Collectanea Botanica* in 1822 by John Lindley who noted that it was based on a plant collected by a Dr Wallich in Nepal.

Description: The arching flowering spikes are up to 25cm (10in) long, each producing three to ten fragrant flowers up to 7.5cm (3in) in diameter. The sepals and petals are a crystalline white and the lip is white with a pale yellow centre. The pseudobulbs are up to 7.5cm (3in) high with two leaves, each up to 25cm (10in) long and 2.5cm (1in) in diameter, protruding from the top. The round bulbs are pale yellow and, with age, tend to form surface indentations.

Flowering season: Winter and spring when the flower spikes appear from the base of the previous season's pseudobulbs.

Cultivation: A medium-grade compost, light shade and cultivation in a cool house environment are required. In winter it should have a dry rest.

Propagation: Like many coelogynes, this plant is best left undisturbed until it grows into a healthy specimen plant.

Synonym: *Cymbidium speciosissimum*.

COELOGYNE ELATA

Native habitat:	This orchid is a native of the Himalayas where it grows at high altitudes.
History:	It was first discovered by Joseph Hooker in Sikkim in 1849.
Description:	The flower spike is up to 60cm (24in) tall and produces four to ten flowers which are up to 5cm (2in) in diameter, long lasting and fragrant. The sepals and petals are white and the lip is white with a yellow throat. The pseudobulbs are up to 12.5cm (5in) tall with two rather tough leaves up to 25cm (10in) long and 5cm (2in) at the top.
Flowering season:	The inflorescence appears from the new growth in the summer, but does not flower until the following spring.
Cultivation:	A medium-grade compost, light shade and cultivation in a cool house are required. Due to the upward growth of the bulbs, this is an ideal orchid for cultivating on a section of bark.

COELOGYNE OCHRACEA

Native habitat: This orchid thrives at high altitudes throughout south-east Asia and the Indian sub-continent.

Description: The flower spikes are up to 20cm (8in) long and each produces six to ten beautifully fragrant, transparent white flowers with an orange-yellow marked lip. The pseudobulbs are a columnar shape, grow to 7.5cm (3in) high and produce two leaves from the top of the bulb which grow to 20cm (8in) long.

Flowering season: The inflorescence appears from new growth in early spring and flowers appear in summer.

Cultivation: A medium-grade compost, light shade and cultivation in a cool house environment are required. As with many coelogynes, this plant is best left undisturbed and is, therefore, ideally suited to potting in a wooden basket suspended from the roof of the greenhouse. In summer it requires light shade and in winter none at all. It also thrives and flowers beautifully if grown indoors in a location that offers a lot of light. Water the plant well (but not over-water) to ensure that when new growths appear and begin to elongate, they do not become covered in a sticky residue which hinders development. In winter this orchid should receive a semi-dry rest.

GOMESA CRISPA

Native habitat:	This orchid is a native of Brazil.
Description:	The flowers are small and delicate, about 1.25cm (½in) in diameter and are green edged with yellow. The pseudobulbs are conical shaped, about 10cm (4in) high and slightly flat in appearance. Each produces two leaves up to 25cm (10in) long from the top of the bulb.
Flowering season:	The flowering season is summer to autumn when stems up to 20cm (8in) long appear from the base of the pseudobulbs and produce many fragrant flowers.
Cultivation:	A medium- to coarse-grade compost, light shade and cultivation in a cool house environment are required. It produces many aerial roots from the base of the pseudobulbs making it an ideal plant for growing on a bark slab or in a wooden basket.
Synonyms:	*Rodriguezia crispa* and *Odontoglossum crispulum*.

MASDEVALLIA GRANULOSA

Native habitat: This orchid is a native of Colombia.

Description: The flowers, which have a very short stem and appear at an angle from the base of the leaves, have a wonderful scent of chocolate. The flowers are approximately 5cm (2in) from tail to tail. The sepals are magenta with tiny, glossy purple spots covering their surface, which give the flowers a 'wet' appearance. The tails are orange, growing paler at the tips.

Flowering season: Spring and summer.

Cultivation: A medium-grade bark compost, medium shade and cultivation in a cool house environment are required.

ODONTOGLOSSUM CRISPUM

Native habitat: This orchid is a native of Colombia where is grows at altitudes of 2,000 to 3,000m (6,600 to 9,900ft) on the western slopes of the Andes.

History: It was first discovered in 1841 near Bogata by Theodore Hartweg.

Description: The flower spikes grow to 40cm (16in) high, each of which produces two to eight flowers. The flowers are predominantly white with some yellow and purple marking around the lip and grow up to 10cm (4in) in diameter. The pseudobulbs grow to 10cm (4in) high and produce five pale green leaves, each up to 40cm (16in) long, two of which protrude from the top of the bulb. With age, the pseudobulbs tend to form surface indentations.

Flowering season: It flowers at any time of year, but most commonly in spring and autumn.

Cultivation: A fine- to medium-grade compost, medium to heavy shade and cultivation in a cool house environment are required.

Points of interest: This is the most favoured Odontoglossum for hybridization; a very high percentage of the Odontoglossum family hybrids have this variety in their genealogy.

ODONTOGLOSSUM HALLII

Native habitat: This orchid is a native of Colombia, Peru and Ecuador where it grows at altitudes of 2,500m (8,250ft).

History: It was discovered by a Colonel Hall in 1837 in Ecuador and is named after him.

Description: The flower spike grows to 80cm (48in) long and produces as many as eighteen flowers which grow to 10cm (4in) in diameter. The sepals, petals and lip of the flower are yellow spotted with reddish brown. The pseudobulbs grow to 10cm (4in) high and produce one or two leaves, each up to 25cm (10in) long which protrude from the top of the bulb.

Flowering season: Spring and summer.

Cultivation: A medium-grade compost, dappled shade and cultivation in a cool house environment are required.

Synonym: *Oncidium Hallii.*

ODONTOGLOSSUM HASTILABIUM

Native habitat: This orchid is a native of Colombia.

History: It was discovered by Jean Linden.

Description: The flower spike arches up to 75cm (30in) in height. The fragrant flowers extend to 7.5cm (3in) in diameter. The sepals and petals are pale green delicately striped with bars of reddish brown while the lip of the flower is lilac. The pseudobulbs grow to 5cm (2in) high and produces one or two leaves, each up to 20cm (8in) long from the top of the bulb.

Flowering season: Summer and autumn.

Cultivation: A medium-grade compost, dappled shade and cultivation in a cool house environment are required.

Points of interest: This plant was transferred to the genus Oncidium by L. Garay and G. C. K. Dunsterville in 1976.

ODONTOGLOSSUM MAJALE

Native habitat: This orchid is a native of Guatemala where it grows at altitudes of 2,500m (8,250ft).

Description: The inflorescence grows to 15cm (6in) tall and produces two to four flowers. These are up to 4cm (1½in) in diameter. The sepals and petals are salmon pink as is the large lip, which is also spotted dark red. The pseudobulbs are up to 7.5cm (3in) high and produce a single leaf, up to 30cm (12in) long, from the top of the bulb.

Flowering season: Spring.

Cultivation: A fine- to medium-grade compost, dappled shade and cultivation in a cool house environment are required.

Synonym: Odontoglossum platycheilum.

ODONTOGLOSSUM TRIUMPHANS

Native habitat:	This orchid is a native of Colombia where it grows in dense forest at altitudes of 1,500 to 3,000m (4,950 to 9,900ft).
Description:	The inflorescence has an arching habit and grows to 80cm (24in) high. It produces abundant flowers, up to 7.5cm (3in) in diameter. The sepals and petals are golden yellow with reddish brown marking, while the lip is yellow and white with a prominent reddish brown marking at the bottom. The pseudobulbs grow to 10cm (4in) high and produce two leaves, each up to 40cm (16in) long, from the top of the bulb.
Flowering season:	Spring.
Cultivation:	A medium-grade compost, dappled shade and cultivation in a cool house environment are required. This orchid first flowers while still a young plant which tends to retard its growth. To resolve this, remove the first year's inflorescence as soon as it appears so that the plant can devote its energy to growing.
Synonym:	*Odontoglossum spectatissimum.*

COELOGYNE OCELLATA

Native habitat: This orchid is a native of the Himalayas where it grows at high altitudes.

Description: Each flower spike produces two to four white flowers with an orange-yellow smudge at the top of the lip. The pseudobulbs are up to 5cm (2in) high and produce two leaves, up to 15cm (6in) long from the top of the bulb.

Flowering season: The flowering season is in winter and spring when the inflorescence appears from the centre of the new growth.

Cultivation: A medium-grade compost, light shade and cultivation in a cool to intermediate house environment are required. In winter, it should receive a dry rest.

Synonyms: *Cymbidium nitidum* and *Coelogyne nitida*. It is also confused with *Coelogyne corymbosa*.

DENDROBIUM INFUNDIBULUM

Native habitat: A native of Thailand and Burma, this plant grows at altitudes of between 1,000 and 2,500m (3,300 to 8,250ft).

Description: Each plant begins as a new growth in spring and grows up to 60cm (24in) high. The canes are covered in small black hairs and produce dark green leaves, up to 7.5cm (3in) long, from joints along its length. The flowers are an ivory white with yellow marking on the throat of the lip, grow up to 10cm (4in) in diameter and last three or four weeks before they begin to wilt. They also each have a spur, up to 2.5cm (1in) long.

Flowering season: The flowering season is spring when one to three flowers are produced from nodes near the top of the newly grown canes and they can also appear on nodes from the previous season's canes.

Cultivation: A medium-grade compost, light shade and cultivation in a cool to intermediate house environment are required.

Synonyms: *Dendrobium moulmeinense.*

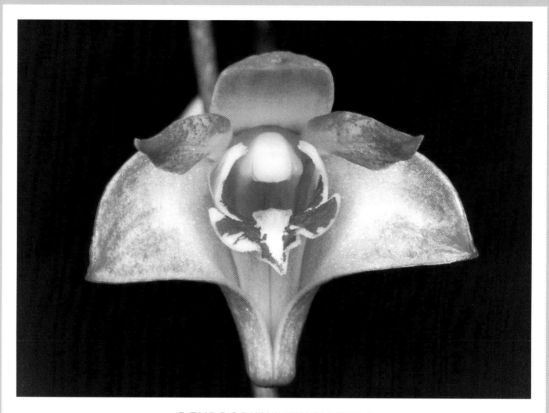

DENDROBIUM KINGIANUM

Native habitat: This orchid is a native of New South Wales in Australia where it grows on rocks.

Description: New growth appears from the previous season's canes and it very quickly becomes a specimen plant. The canes are cylindrical and up to 25cm (10in) tall, producing up to six leaves each 10cm (4in) long. Each inflorescence is up to 15cm (6in) long and produces up to twelve gently fragrant flowers, approximately 2cm (¾in) in diameter, which vary from plant to plant, but are usually either white, pink or purple.

Flowering season: The flowering season is winter and early spring when one to three flower spikes appear from the top of each cane.

Cultivation: A medium-grade compost, light shade and cultivation in a cool to intermediate house environment is required. This orchid is hardy, prolific and always grows well. It is ideally suited to growing in a basket suspended from the roof of the greenhouse although as the plant grows, it can become very heavy. It is also easy to grow indoors in a light, airy location.

Synonym: *Callista kingianum.*

DENDROBIUM THYRSIFLORUM

Native habitat: This orchid is a native of Burma, Thailand and the Himalayas.

Description: The canes of this plant are up to 50cm (20in) tall and produce three to five leaves from the apex, each up to 15cm (6in) long. They have a furrowed, slightly shrivelled appearance. The pendulous inflorescence, up to 25cm (10in) high, produces abundant flowers which grow to 5cm (2in) in diameter. The sepals and petals are white with a deep orange-yellow lip. The edge of the lip is fimbriated giving the flower a 'fluffy' appearance.

Flowering season: The flowering season is spring when flower spikes appear from nodes near the top of the newly grown canes. They can also appear from the previous season's canes.

Cultivation: A medium- to coarse-grade compost, light shade and cultivation in a cool to intermediate house environment are required. During the growing period, it should have a warm, moist environment, but in winter, it should receive a cool, dry rest.

Synonyms: *Dendrobium amabile* and *Callista amabilis*.

ENCYCLIA COCHLEATA

Native habitat: This orchid is a native of Florida, Mexico and the West Indies and is also found in southern regions of Central America, for example Venezuela. It thrives in mixed forest at altitudes of 2,000m (6,600ft).

Description: The inflorescence is up to 50cm (20in) long and produces abundant flowers.The sepals and petals are a pale green and the uppermost lip is a yellow-green with deep purple veins and markings. The pseudobulbs are pear-shaped and up to 25cm (10in) high and each produces two or three leaves, up to 30cm (12in) long, at the top.

Flowering season: The flowering season lasts almost the whole year and it is possible for a large plant to be in perpetual bloom.

Cultivation: A medium-grade compost, light to medium shade and cultivation in a cool to intermediate house are required.

Propagation: This plant is easy to propagate from back bulbs.

Synonyms: Due to the shape of its lip, this orchid is often referred to as the 'Cockleshell Orchid'. More formally, it is also known as *Epidendrum cochleatum*, *Anacheilium cochleatum* and *Phaedrosanthus cochleatus*.

MASDEVALLIA AMABILIS

Native habitat: This orchid is a native of Peru where it grows in the Andes at high altitudes.

Description: The flowers are up to 2.5cm (1in) in diameter, 5cm (2in) in length, and are magenta with red veins and orange-yellow tails. It produces leathery leaves up to 15cm (6in) long. It produces no pseudobulbs and should, therefore, never be allowed to dry out.

Flowering season: The flowering season is winter when single-flowered spikes up to 25cm (10in) long appear from the base of the leaves.

Cultivation: A medium-grade compost, light shade and cultivation in a cool to intermediate house environment are required.

ODONTOGLOSSUM BICTONIENSE

Native habitat: This orchid is a native of Mexico, El Salvador and Guatemala where it grows at altitudes of 1,500 to 3,200m (4,950 to 10,560ft).

History: It first flowered in Britain at Bicton in Devon as part of the collection of Lord Rolle and was subsequently named after the estate.

Description: Flower spikes grow to 1m (3½ft) high, each producing up to forty flowers, 5cm (2in) in diameter. The sepals and petals are green with brown markings and the lip can be a range of colours, from white to cerise. The pseudobulbs grow to 15cm (6in) high, each producing up to seven leaves which are 40cm (16in) long.

Flowering season: Summer and autumn.

Cultivation: A coarse-grade compost, light to medium shade and cultivation in a cool to intermediate house environment are required. The variety 'alba' has paler leaves and is not so vigorous. It willingly flowers indoors, making it a popular orchid to grow as a houseplant.

Propagation: New growths often appear from old bulbs giving multiple leads, which means that a specimen plant is easy to cultivate.

ODONTOGLOSSUM CERVANTESII

Native habitat: This orchid is a native of Mexico and Guatemala where it grows at altitudes of 1,500 to 3,000m (4,950 to 9,900ft).

History: It was named after Vincentio Cervantes, the Mexican botanist who discovered it.

Description: Flower spikes grow to 30cm (12in) long, each producing up to five flowers. The flowers are up to 5cm (2in) in diameter and have white sepals. The petals are also white with brown rings around the centre. The lip is white with a golden yellow smudge at the top. Each pseudobulb grows to 6cm (2⅓in) and produces a single leaf up to 15cm (6in) in length from the top of the bulb. This plant grows and flowers well indoors.

Flowering season: Winter and spring.

Cultivation: Medium shade, a fine- to medium-grade compost and cultivation in a cool to intermediate house environment are required.

ODONTOGLOSSUM CORDATUM

Native habitat: This orchid originates from Mexico and many other parts of Central America.

Description: The flower spike blossom in the spring following its appearance from the base of the newly grown pseudobulb the previous autumn. The inflorescence is up to 60cm (24in) long and has an arching habit. It produces up to twelve flowers, each of which grows to 7.5cm (3in) in diameter. The flowers are yellow with heavy brown markings, while the lip has white markings near the top. The pseudobulbs are up to 7.5cm (3in) high and produces up to six bright green leaves approximately 30cm (12in) long, one or two protruding from the top of the bulb. Each pseudobulb grows slightly higher than its predecessor making this plant ideal for cultivating on bark or in a wooden basket.

Flowering season: Spring.

Cultivation: The plant's thick roots, some of which are aerial, require a medium- to coarse-grade compost, light to medium shade and cultivation in a cool to intermediate house environment.

ODONTOGLOSSUM LAEVE

Native habitat: This orchid is a native of Mexico and Guatemala where it grows at altitudes as high as 1,600m (5,280ft).

Description: The inflorescence grows to 1m (3⅓ft) in height and produces many branches. The flowers are scented and grow to 7.5cm (3in) in diameter. The sepals and petals are yellow-green delicately striped with purplish brown bars while the lip is dark lilac graduating to pale lilac at the bottom. The pseudobulbs grow to 10cm (4in) high and produce two leaves, each up to 45cm (18in), from the top of the bulb. This plant requires a hard rest, i.e. no water, when the bulbs are fully grown to ensure a successful flowering season. With age, they tend to form surface indentations.

Flowering season: Spring.

Cultivation: A medium-grade compost, dappled shade and cultivation in a cool to intermediate house environment are required.

ODONTOGLOSSUM ROSSII

Native habitat: This orchid is a native of Guatemala, Mexico, Honduras and Nicaragua where it grows at altitudes of 3,000m (9,900ft).

Description: The inflorescence grows to 20cm (8in) high and produces two to five flowers, each of which grows to 7.5cm (3in) in diameter. The petals and lip are white, while the sepals are white with brown spotting. With specific varieties, the lip can also be pink. The pseudobulbs grow to 5cm (2in) in height and produce a single leaf, up to 20cm (8in) long, from the top of the bulb.

Flowering season: Winter.

Cultivation: A fine- to medium-grade compost, dappled shade and cultivation in a cool to intermediate house environment is required. This plant grows well as an indoor plant.

Propagation: It is relatively easy to grow this variety into a specimen plant.

Synonyms: *Odontoglossum caerulescens, Odontoglossum rubescens, Odontoglossum Warnerianum, Odontoglossum Youngii* and *Odontoglossum Dawsonianum.*

ODONTOGLOSSUM STELLATUM

Native habitat:	This orchid is a native of Guatemala and Mexico where it grows on the tree moss.
Description:	The inflorescence grows to 15cm (6in) tall and produces one or two star-shaped flowers, each approximately 4cm (1½in) in diameter. The sepals and petals are light brown with yellow edges while the lip is dark lilac graduating to pale lilac at the edge. The pseudobulbs grow to 5cm (2in) in height and produce a single leaf, up to 15cm (6in) long, from the top of the bulb.
Flowering season:	Winter.
Cultivation:	A fine-grade compost, dappled shade and cultivation in a cool to intermediate house environment are required.
Synonyms:	*Odontoglossum erosum* and *Oncidium erosum*.

ONCIDIUM LONGIPES

Native habitat: This orchid is a native of Brazil.

Description: The inflorescence can grow to 15cm (6in) long. Each spike produces three to five long-lasting flowers, each measuring up to 3.5cm (1½in) in diameter. The sepals and petals are yellow-green and the lip is yellow with reddish brown markings. The pseudobulbs are up to 2.5cm (1in) high and with age tend to form surface indentations. They produce two leaves, each measuring up to 15cm (6in) long, from the top of the bulb.

Flowering season: Spring.

Cultivation: A fine-grade compost, light shade and cultivation in a cool to intermediate house environment are required. This plant is ideally suited to growing on a bark slab where it quickly becomes a specimen plant.

ONCIDIUM ORNITHORYNCHUM

Native habitat: This orchid is a native of several South American countries including Guatemala, El Salvador, Costa Rica and Mexico.

Description: Each pseudobulb produces at least two inflorescences. These grow to 30cm (12in) long and have many branches which produce abundant flowers. The flowers are fragrant, approximately 2cm (¾in) long and are lilac with yellow marking at the top of the lip. The pseudobulbs grow to 6cm (2½in) and produce two leaves, each up to 20cm (8in) long, from the top of the bulb.

Flowering season: Autumn.

Cultivation: A fine-grade compost, light shade and cultivation in a cool to intermediate house environment is required. It should be given a short dry rest in winter.

Points of interest: This plant's name comes from the Greek for 'bird beak' which refers to the shape of the rostellum.

ONCIDIUM RANIFERUM

Native habitat: This orchid is a native of Brazil.

Description: The inflorescence, which grows to 30cm (12in) high, has several branches and produces abundant flowers. The flowers are 1.5cm (⅝in) long, bright yellow with orange-red markings at the top of the lip. The pseudobulbs grow to 5cm (2in) high and produce two leaves, each up to 15cm (6in) long, from the top of the bulb. With age, they tend to form surface indentations.

Flowering season: Spring.

Cultivation: A fine- to medium-grade compost, light shade and cultivation in a cool to intermediate house environment are required. Although the flowers are tiny, they grow in abundance making this a very attractive plant for the greenhouse and an ideal houseplant.

ONCIDIUM TIGRINUM

Native habitat: This orchid is a native of Mexico where it grows at altitudes of 2,000 to 2,500m (6,600 to 8,250ft).

Description: Several inflorescences grow to 90cm (36in) high and produce abundant flowers. The flowers grow to 7.5cm (3in) long and are very fragrant. The sepals and petals are yellow striped with bars of brown and the larger lip is bright yellow. The pseudobulbs grow to 10cm (4in) high and produce two or three leaves from the top of the bulb, each of which grows to 40cm (16in) long.

Flowering season: Autumn.

Cultivation: A medium-grade compost, light shade and cultivation in a cool to intermediate house environment are required. It should be given a rest in winter.

Synonyms: *Oncidium unguiculatum* and *Odontoglossum tigrinum*.

OSMOGLOSSUM PULCHELLUM

Native habitat: This orchid is a native of several South American countries including Guatemala, Costa Rica, Mexico and El Salvador, where it grows at altitudes of 2,500m (8,250ft).

Description: The flower spikes appear from the base of the bulb in winter. They grow to 50cm (20in) long and produce six to ten flowers. The flowers are up to 2cm (¾in) in diameter and are white with a yellow smudge at the uppermost part of the lip. The pseudobulbs grow to 10cm (4in) tall and produce two leaves, each measuring to 30cm (12in) long, from the top of the bulb.

Flowering season: Spring.

Cultivation: A fine-grade compost, dappled shade and cultivation in a cool to intermediate house environment is required.

Synonym: *Odontoglossum pulchellum.*

Points of interest: This orchid is often called the 'Lily of the Valley orchid' because of its powerful scent.

PAPHIOPEDILUM VILLOSUM

Native habitat: This orchid is a native of India, Thailand and Burma and grows at altitudes of 1,000m (3,300ft) and above.

Description: The inflorescence grows to 17.5cm (7in) high and is covered with long, dark purple hairs. It produces flowers up to 15cm (6in) in diameter which have a glossy, 'varnished' appearance. The dorsal sepal is green with white edges and brown markings. The petals are light brown and the pouch is a light brown and orange-yellow on the inside. The flowers normally last as long as eight weeks. New growth appears in autumn, producing leaves up to 40cm (16in) long.

Flowering season: Winter.

Cultivation: A fine- to medium-grade compost, dappled to heavy shade and cultivation in a cool to intermediate house environment are required. This variety of Paphiopedilums is very easy to cultivate and is, therefore, a good variety for beginners to orchid growing.

Synonym: *Cypripedium villosum*.

ROSSIOGLOSSUM GRANDE

Native habitat: This orchid is a native of Mexico and Guatemala where it grows at altitudes of over 2,700m (8,910ft).

History: It was discovered in 1839 by George Ure Skinner, a professional plant hunter, who sent samples to plant collector, James Bateman. It first flowered in Britain in 1841 at Woburn Abbey.

Description: Two flower spikes appear from the base of the bulb in summer and can grow to a height of 30cm (12in). They each produce two to six flowers which grow to 15cm (6in) in diameter and have a waxy, artificial appearance. The petals are reddish brown at the centre fading to yellow at the tips. The pseudobulbs grow to 10cm (4in) high and produce two or three thick, dark green leaves up to 30cm (12in) long from the top of the bulb. The underside of the leaves are speckled light brown which can be mistaken for red spider mite damage.

Flowering season: In ideal conditions it flowers twice a year, but if it flowers only once it is in autumn.

Cultivation: This plant requires a less humid environment than other orchids and also appreciates lots of light, therefore in summer it should be grown in a cool to intermediate house environment and positioned in light shade; in winter it should have no shade at all. Ideally, it should be potted in coarse-grade bark compost in a wooden basket to accommodate its thick roots and suspended from the roof of the greenhouse in order to gain the best light and drier air. It should receive a dry rest in winter. It is ideally suited to growing indoors as a houseplant.

Synonym: The very centre of the flower contorts to affect a shape and character not unlike that of a clown, which explains its common name: 'Clown orchid'.

SYMPHYGLOSSUM SANGUINEUM

Native habitat: This orchid is a native of Equador.

Description: The inflorescence grows to 50cm (20in) long and produces abundant flowers from several branches. The long-lasting flowers grow to a mere 2cm (¾in) in diameter and are bright red. The lip has white markings at the top. The flowers do not fully open so the lip is often partially obscured by the sepals and petals. The pseudobulbs grow to 5cm (2in) high and produce one or two leaves up to 20cm (8in) long.

Flowering season: Autumn and spring.

Cultivation: A fine- to medium-grade compost, dappled shade and cultivation in a cool to intermediate house environment are required.

Synonyms: *Mesopinidium cochliodum* and *Cochlioda sanguinea*.

THUNIA MARSHALLIANA

Native habitat: This orchid is a native of Burma, China and Thailand.

Description: The flowers are up to 10cm (4in) in diameter. The sepals and petals are white and the fringed lip is white with an orange-red centre. The stems are up to 1.2m (4½ft) tall with pale glaucous leaves which emerge from joints along the entire length. Offsets appear at the top of the stems and, once these have roots, they can be severed and potted to increase stocks of the plant.

Flowering season: Summer when the inflorescence appears from the top of the stems and produces up to ten flowers.

Cultivation: A fine- to medium-grade compost, medium shade and and cultivation in a cool to intermediate house environment are required. This plant should be given a hard rest from the time the leaves drop until new growth appears.

VANDA CRISTATA

Native habitat: This orchid is a native of Nepal, Bhutan and India (Sikkim) where it grows at high altitudes.

Description: The flowers are long-lasting, fragrant, up to 5cm (2in) in diameter and have yellow-green sepals and petals, a white lip and dark red marking. The stems are up to 15cm (6in) tall, with stiff, leathery leaves each up to 15cm (6in) long.

Cultivation: A medium-grade compost, light shade and cultivation in a cool to intermediate house environment are required. This orchid is ideally suited to growing in a wooden basket or on a bark slab.

Synonyms: *Vanda striata* and *Aerides cristatum*.

ASPASIA LUNATA

Native habitat: This epiphytic orchid originates from Brazil where it grows on trees from sea level to over 1,000m (3,300ft).

Description: The inflorescence is up to 7.5cm (3in) tall and produces one or two flowers which are fragrant, long lasting and up to 4cm (1½in) in height. The sepals and petals are light green with purplish brown mottling, while the lip is white with a violet stain towards the centre. The pseudobulbs are up to 5cm (2in) in height, and produce one or two leaves up to 20cm (8in) long from the top of the bulb.

Flowering season: Spring.

Cultivation: A medium-grade compost, dappled shade and cultivation in an intermediate house environment are required.

Synonyms: *Odontoglossum lunatum* and *Trophianthus zonatus*.

COELOGYNE MOOREANA 'CRAGGWOOD'

Native habitat: This orchid is a native of Vietnam where it grows at altitudes of 1,200m (3,960ft).

History: It was named after F. W. Moore of the Glasnevin Botanic Gardens in Dublin.

Description: The inflorescence is up to 50cm (20in) tall and produces four to eight fragrant flowers, each up to 10cm (4in) in diameter. The sepals and petals are transparent white and the lip is white with a yellow and orange smudge in the centre. The pseudobulbs are up to 7.5cm (3in) high which, with age, tend to form surface indentations. They produce two thick, glossy leaves, each up to 40cm (16in) long and 2.5cm (1in) in diameter, which protrude from the top of the bulbs.

Flowering season: Spring and summer.

Cultivation: A medium- to coarse-grade compost, light to dappled shade and cultivation in an intermediate house environment are required.

DENDROBIUM BELLATULUM

Native habitat: This orchid is a native of Burma, China, Thailand and Vietnam where it grows at altitudes of 1,000 to 1,500m (3,300 to 4,950ft).

Description: The flowers are fragrant and up to 3cm (1¼in) in diameter. The sepals and petals are white and the lip is yellow with a deep red smudge near the centre. The canes are up to 6cm (2½in) tall with two leaves protruding from the top which are up to 5cm (2in) long and covered in short, black hairs.

Flowering season: The flowering season is in spring when one to three flowers appear on a short inflorescence from nodes near the top of the cane.

Cultivation: A medium- to coarse-grade compost, light shade and cultivation in an intermediate house environment are required. This plant can be successfully grown on cork bark.

ONCIDIUM FLEXUOSUM

Native habitat: This orchid is a native of Brazil, Paraguay, Argentina and Uruguay.

Description: The inflorescence has an arching habit, grows to 1m (3⅓ft) and produces an abundance of flowers. The flowers are tiny, only 2.5cm (1in) in diameter. The small sepals and petals are golden yellow with reddish brown markings, while the comparatively large lip is yellow with reddish brown markings towards the centre. The pseudobulbs are up to 7.5cm (3in) high and produce two leaves, each up to 30cm (12in) long, at the top of the bulb.

Flowering season: Autumn and winter.

Cultivation: A medium-grade compost, dappled shade and cultivation in an intermediate house environment are required.

Synonyms: *Oncidium haematochrysum, Oncidium haematoxanthum* and *Epidendrum lineatum*.

ONCIDIUM INCURVUM

Native habitat: This orchid is a native of Mexico where it grows at altitudes of 1,000 to 1,500m (3,300 to 4,950ft).

Description: This plant produces several inflorescences, each up to 1.5m (5ft) long. The flowers are white striped with bars of violet, up to 2.5cm (1in) in diameter with twisted sepals and petals. The flowers on this plant are very slow to open; they can take up to a year to bloom from the appearance of the inflorescence. The pseudobulbs are up to 10cm (4in) high and, with age, tend to form surface indentations. They produce two leaves, each up to 40cm (16in) long from the top of the bulb and several additional leaves from the base of the bulb.

Flowering season: Autumn.

Cultivation: A fine- to medium-grade compost, light shade and cultivation in an intermediate house environment are required. The plant will need to be well watered in summer and given little in winter. It grows well indoors and makes an ideal houseplant.

ENCYCLIA PENTOTIS

Native habitat: This orchid thrives in the region stretching from Mexico to Colombia.

Flowering season: The flowering season is late spring to early summer when two flowers appear, back to back, from the top of the pseudobulbs.

Description: The sepals and petals are ivory white while the lip is also white with dark red or purple veins radiating from the centre. The flowers are up to 7.5cm (3in) in diameter, have virtually no stem and are very fragrant. The pseudobulbs form into a slight club-shape and grow up to 40cm (16in) long. Each produces two rather tough leaves from the top, measuring up to 30cm (12in) long.

Cultivation: A medium-grade bark compost and light to medium shade. This orchid is unusually accommodating and thrives in a cool, intermediate or warm house environment. Its long, narrow shape is ideally suited to growth in a wooden basket suspended from the roof of the greenhouse. It should receive a semi-dry rest in winter.

Synonyms: *Epidendrum baculus, Epidendrum fragrans, Epidendrum acuminatum, Epidendrum beyrodtianum, Epidendrum confusum* and *Encyclia baculus.*

ENCYCLIA RADIATA

Native habitat: This orchid can be found in a number of South American countries, including Hondurus, Costa Rica, Guatemala and Mexico where it grows in mixed forest at altitudes of 200 to 2,000m (660 to 6,600ft).

Description: Each flower spike contains four to eight thickly textured, fragrant flowers. The sepals and petals are ivory and the lip is ivory with dark red veins radiating from the centre. Like other members of the encyclia family, the pseudobulbs are club-shaped in appearance. They grow to 10cm (4in) in height and each produces two leaves from the top of the bulb which grow to 25cm (10in) long.

Flowering season: The flowering season is summer to autumn when an inflorescence up to 17.5cm (7in) long appears from the top of the pseudobulb.

Cultivation: A medium-grade compost and light shade are required. Like the *Encyclia pentotis*, it thrives in cool and warm growing conditions.

Synonyms: *Epidendrum radiatum* and *Epidendrum marginatum*.

EPIDENDRUM IBAGUENSE

Native habitat: This orchid originates from Mexico and throughout the tropical South American countries where it is found growing in soil and on rocks.

Description: In its natural environment, the stems or canes grow to a staggering 10m (33ft), but under greenhouse conditions, more commonly to 1m (3⅓ft). It produces an abundance of flowers which form into a tight bloom, up to 4cm (1½in) in diameter, and is available in a range of colours including magenta, yellow, orange and white. The leaves are fleshy and grow to 10cm (4in) long. Aerial roots and new growths appear from the leaf joints.

Flowering season: This plant flowers throughout the year and a specimen plant can be in perpetual bloom.

Cultivation: A medium- to coarse-grade compost, full sun and cultivation in a wide range of growing conditions is acceptable. Due to its growing habit and large numbers of aerial roots this plant is not suitable for growing indoors. The variety 'schomburgkii', which has large, brick red flowers, is a popular variety for cultivation.

Synonyms: *Epidendrum pratense, Epidendrum radicans, Epidendrum rhizophorum, Epidendrum calanthum, Epidendrum decipiens* and *Epidendrum fulgens*.

FURTHER READING & USEFUL ADDRESSES

BOOKS

Bechtel/Cribb/Launert, *The Manual of Cultivated Orchid Species*, Blandford Press, Poole, Dorset, 1986. ISBN 0 7137 16282

McKenzie Black, Peter, *Orchids*, Hamlyn, London, 1983. ISBN 0 600 368874

Bockemühl, Leonore, *Odontoglossum*, Brücke-Verlag Kurt Schmersow, Hildesheim, Germany, 1989. ISBN 387105 0237

Bristow, Alec, *Orchids*, Wisley Handbook 42, Royal Horticultural Society, London, 1982. ISBN 0 906 603234

Davidson, William, *The Illustrated Directory of House Plants*, Salamander, London, 1983. ISBN 0 861 011716

Dressler, Robert L, *The Orchids: Natural History and Classification*, Harvard University Press, London, 1981. ISBN 0 674 875257

Hawkes, Alex D, *Encyclopedia of Cultivated Orchids*, Faber & Faber, London, 1987 ISBN 0 571 065023

Rittershausen, B & W, *Orchids in Colour*, Blandford Press, Poole, Dorset, 1979 ISBN 0 713 70859X

Rittershausen, B & W, *Orchid Growing Illustrated*, Blandford Press, Poole, Dorset, 1985. ISBN 0 713 713658

Rittershausen, B & W, *Orchids as Indoor Plants*, Blandford Press, Poole, Dorset, 1980 ISBN 0 713 709987

Williams, B, *Orchids for Everyone*, Salamander, London, 1980. ISBN 0 861 010353

N.B. If you find that any of the above are out of print, try your local library or second-hand bookshops.

UK ADDRESSES

The British Orchid Growers Association
Plested Orchids, 38 Florence Road
College Town, Sandhurst, Berkshire GU47 0QD
Contact: Janet Plested
Telephone: 01276 32947

The Orchid Society of Great Britain
Athelney, 145 Binscombe Village
Godalming, Surrey GU7 3QL
Contact: Mrs Betty Arnold
Telephone: 01483 421423

The Royal Botanic Gardens
Kew, Richmond, Surrey TW9 3AB
Contact: Sandra Bell
Telephone: 0181 332 5564
Fax: 0181 332 5197

The Royal Horticultural Society
The R.H.S. Garden, Wisley
Woking, Surrey GU23 6QB
Contact: The Director of Horticulture
Telephone: 01483 22423

USA ADDRESS

American Orchid Society
6000 South Olive Avenue, West Palm Beach
FL 33405. Email: TheAOS@compuserve.com

AUSTRALIA CONTACT

Email: graemebr@ozemail.com.au

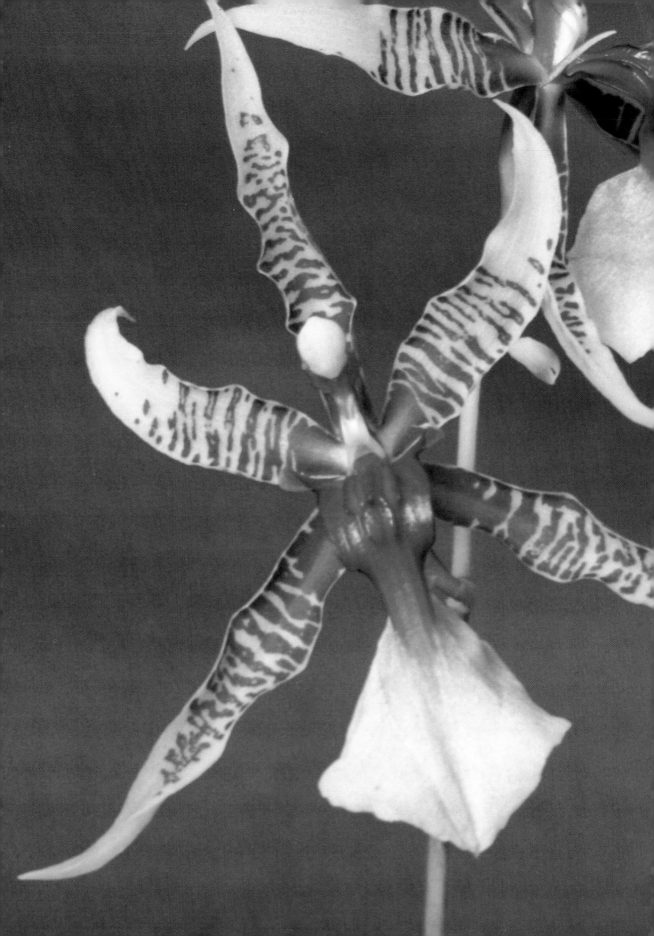

ABOUT THE AUTHOR

TOM Gilland was introduced to gardening at a very young age by his grandfather and has been passionate about it ever since.

In 1981, returning to Scotland from a period living in Canada, he transformed a small, undeveloped garden into a beautiful plant-filled environment. This success inspired an interest in houseplants, and specifically, orchids, of which Tom now has a collection of over 100 varieties.

Tom has been a member of, and gained prizes from, the Scottish Orchid Society and the Orchid Society of Great Britain for his photographs of orchids and has recently completed an RHS General Certificate in Horticulture. He is currently pursuing an interest in hydroponics.

INDEX

INDEX